A RUSSIAN TRILOGY

T0347817

Reza de Wet

A RUSSIAN TRILOGY

THREE SISTERS TWO
YELENA
ON THE LAKE

OBERON BOOKS

LONDON

First published in this collection in 2002 by Oberon Books Ltd.
(incorporating Absolute Classics)
521 Caledonian Road, London N7 9RH
Tel: +44 (0) 20 7607 3637 / Fax: +44 (0) 20 7607 3629
e-mail: info@oberonbooks.com
www.oberonbooks.com

Reprinted in 2005

Copyright © Reza de Wet, 2002
Copyright introduction © Reza de Wet, 2002

Reza de Wet is hereby identified as author of these works in
accordance with section 77 of the Copyright, Designs and
Patents Act 1988. The author has asserted her moral rights.

All rights whatsoever in these plays are strictly reserved and
application for performance etc. should be made before rehearsal
to Gordon Dickerson, 2 Crescent Grove, London SW4 7AH. No
performance may be given unless a licence has been obtained,
and no alterations may be made in the title or the text of the play
without the author's prior written consent.

You may not copy, store, distribute, transmit, reproduce or
otherwise make available this publication (or any part of it) in
any form, or binding or by any means (print, electronic, digital,
optical, mechanical, photocopying, recording or otherwise),
without the prior written permission of the publisher. Any person
who does any unauthorized act in relation to this publication may
be liable to criminal prosecution and civil claims for damages.

A catalogue record for this book is available from the British Library.

PB ISBN: 978-1-84002-168-4
E ISBN: 978-1-78319-474-2

Cover illustration: Andrzej Klimowski

Visit www.oberonbooks.com to read more about all our books
and to buy them. You will also find features, author interviews and
news of any author events, and you can sign up for e-newsletters
so that you're always first to hear about our new releases.

Contents

Introduction, 7

THREE SISTERS TWO, 15

YELENA, 95

ON THE LAKE, 167

Acknowledgements

For their encouragement and support, my heartful thanks to Gordon Dickerson, Marthinus Basson, Mannie Manin, Lynette Marais and Gary Gordon. I owe a special debt of gratitude to Lindsay Reardon, for his tireless and expert advice during the writing of these playtexts.

Introduction

Reza de Wet in conversation with Juanita Perez

Juanita Perez is an academic, a lecturer, an actress and an innovative choreographer. Her previous interview with Reza de Wet was published in 'Contemporary Theatre Review' and edited by Mary Malley.

Juanita: About six years ago you mentioned that you were working on a series of texts in response to Chekhov's major plays. This would be your third series of plays. The first cycle of the three plays which the critics labelled as 'comic-gothic' examined the politics of violence and oppression within the family and the second cycle of plays was concerned with finding a synthesis between the magical, the naive and the grotesque. Am I right?

Reza: Yes, in essence.

Juanita: Why are you drawn to writing series of plays?

Reza: It gives me the opportunity to create texts which on the one hand function entirely independently but which in conjunction can present constantly shifting perspectives. The crucial factor is transformation while, at the same time, there is the sense of an enduring unifying element.

Juanita: Why Chekhov?

Reza: I suppose on the simplest level these plays, speaking so poignantly of a vanishing order, reflected my situation as a 'privileged' Afrikaaner standing on the threshold of far-reaching socio-political change. I could identify with these characters who sense that their existence is precarious and morally flawed.

Juanita: And on another level?

Reza: I was excited by the thought of examining style, form and content in relation to these texts.

Juanita: How did you begin the process of writing *Three Sisters Two*? Did you have a particular approach?

Reza: Yes. To begin with, I decided to superimpose two Chekhov texts in order to present a more composite image of dispossession.

Juanita: *Three Sisters* is obviously the one play, which is the other?

Reza: *The Cherry Orchard.*

Juanita: Why these two plays?

Reza: They both deal with diminishing circumstances, loss and – particularly *The Cherry Orchard* – with devastating and irrevocable change.

Juanita: How did you go about 'superimposing' these two texts without creating complete confusion?

Reza: I used my own 'distilled' version of the characters from *Three Sisters* but took elements of the plot, structure, tone and rhythm from *The Cherry Orchard*.

Juanita: Please explain.

Reza: First the plot. Of course, *Three Sisters Two* approximates *The Cherry Orchard* only in broad outlines. Both plays start with an arrival which in some sense seems to precipitate a crisis. In *The Cherry Orchard* it is Madame Ranevskaya and in *Three Sisters Two*, Masha. Both women have become sophisticated city dwellers involved in illicit affairs. The subsequent action in both plays unfolds in relation to an impending crisis which threatens to disrupt and destroy their old way of life. Events come to a head in both *The Cherry Orchard* and *Three Sisters Two* – during Act Three while the sounds of a ball in progress can be heard off stage. *Three Sisters Two*, like *The Cherry Orchard*, ends with a departure scene as, amidst luggage and the confusion of last farewells, the characters have to come to terms with irretrievable loss. In *The Cherry Orchard* an old family retainer, Feers, is forgotten in the empty house. In *Three Sisters Two* it is the Prozorov's old nanny, Anfisa. *The Cherry Orchard* ends with the sound of beautiful old cherry trees being chopped down, while *Three Sisters Two* ends with the sounds of gunfire and explosions signifying the approach of the victorious Red Army. While there is a sense, in *The Cherry Orchard* of Lopakhin's haste to claim the estate on which his father had been a serf, in *Three Sisters Two* it is the peasants inhabiting the rest of the house, gleefully waiting to take possession of the domain that belonged to the 'gentry'. As far as the structure is concerned, both plays start with an arrival scene leading to a rather restless coming and going and with the upheaval of a departure amidst fervent activity. In both cases Act Two is more quiet and lyrical and takes place at dusk. In *The Cherry Orchard* the action is set near the river. In *Three Sisters Two* the action, although confined to the nursery, centres around the character's movements to and from the river. Act Three, for both plays, starts fairly quietly, but reaches a feverish climax, juxtaposed by the mindless jollity of a ball taking place offstage.

Juanita: You mentioned using the tone and rhythm of *The Cherry Orchard*. Can you elaborate on that?

Reza: Yes. I felt that the more melancholy, elegiac tone and rhythm of *Three Sisters* combined with the subject of war and devastation would become too oppressive. For me *The Cherry Orchard* is a sublime example of an effective contrast between rhythm, tempo and content. Writing about a profoundly poignant subject, Chekhov boldly created – in *The Cherry Orchard* – what he describes as 'a play which is entirely happy and frivolous...a comedy... almost a farce'. To emphasise the quick, comic, farcical tempo, he insisted that Act Three is 'an Act which should last a maximum of twelves minutes'. Following his example I found that a lighter tone threw the more ominous aspects of *Three Sisters Two* into much more effective relief.

Juanita: I suppose an analogy for the cherry trees could be found in the Prozorov's ruined garden and in the birch trees being chopped down for firewood.

Reza: Yes.

Juanita: It also strikes me that the eerie sound in Act Two of a church bell ringing as it falls to the ground could evoke the mysterious sound of 'the broken string' in Act Two of *The Cherry Orchard*?

Reza: Yes. I looked for something to correspond with that. When I discovered, during my research, that church bells had been cut down and used for ammunition, I felt that I'd found what I needed.

Juanita: I remember being present at the first performance of *Three Sisters Two*. Of course it was performed in

Afrikaans. I was entirely absorbed by the action and – on a conscious level – I wasn't aware of all these interconnecting strands that you've talked about.

Reza: That's what I tried to achieve. These allusions should simply 'shine through' the surface of an original and self sufficient text.

Juanita: So, in a sense, your own text would then be the third text in this trinity?

Reza: That's right. It would also reflect my own personal experience as an Afrikaner. But I could not simply construct a narrative and impose it on the other texts. In order to resonate with the other texts, my play also had to be musically patterned, atmospheric and achieve a fine balance between comedy and pathos. This could not be done by simply 'imitating' a Chekhov text (something which, happily, I don't think is possible). In order to create a text which was as 'authentic' as the two intertexts, I had to enter into the experience in a very personal way in order to hear my own music and find my own meaning. I was very pleased with the way the audience reacted to the play when it was performed here. They laughed uproariously and were very moved, mainly because they were convinced that the play was 'about us'.

Juanita: The next play in the series is a much darker play. There is a significant tonal shift.

Reza: *Uncle Vanya* is a more concentrated play than *Three Sisters* or *The Cherry Orchard* in terms of having fewer characters. That, and the highly charged atmosphere, has always reminded me of Ibsen's dramas of domestic desolation and incarceration with their sense of emotional turbulence under the surface and an almost unbearable tension between the sexes. I decided to explore this correspondence by cutting down the cast of the play, *Yelena*, to five characters by attempting to create a feeling of extreme claustrophobia and by using a structure that is not Chekhovian. In Chekhov a few characters share our equal attention and the interaction between these characters create the fabric of the play. I decided to use the Ibsen 'model' where a central character, such as Hedda Gabler, becomes a vortex which the other characters circle around. And as far as the tone is concerned, I concentrated on dense, dark, sombre colours instead of Chekhov's shimmering, subtle washes of colour. Instead of comedy and pathos, the humour in *Yelena* is very black and apart from empathising with the characters I also wanted the audience to experience a certain horror as the ghastly logic of the character's fears and obsession are revealed. Lastly, the rhythm of *Yelena* differs completely from the musical, more harmonious quality of Chekhov's plays. In *Yelena* the 'music' is more discordant, erratic and tempestuous as reflected by the disturbing Scriabin music Yelena plays at the end of Act Three.

Juanita: The entire play takes place at night. This is strangely disturbing. I suppose that is what you intended?

Reza: Yes. I wanted this perpetual darkness to reflect the 'underworld' of obsession and compulsion.

Juanita: This leads me to the themes. Decay seems to be a very important theme and you deal with it in a graphic way. There is the old house with 'death watch' beetles in the walls, the rotting hay, the cholera epidemic, Telegin's gagga, toothless old wife, the blind, old nanny who is waiting to die in her small, dark room and of course, Yelena who is being ravaged by a fatal disease. And then, Astrov, Vanya and Sonja have such a desperate need for Yelena that they seem to be draining her of her life blood. This strongly suggests vampirism, as Yelena points out. This is emphasised when, towards the end of Act Two, the two men look down at the drugged, unconscious Yelena who is lying at their feet, while they discuss ways of trapping her so that she can serve their needs. I also find the image at the end of the Act rather disquieting. Astrov carrying the unconscious Yelena to her bed. These dark themes are certainly not typical of a Chekhov play. In fact, these themes seem to reflect the concerns of the Symbolists.

Reza: I believe that these themes are present in *Uncle Vanya*. But very submerged. In a sense, *Yelena* is the 'shadow' of *Uncle Vanya*.

Juanita: Yes. I know what you mean. On the one hand
Yelena seems quite Chekhovian. And yet there is
something much more ominous about the play. It seems
to exist simultaneously on two levels.

Reza: I wanted the windows covering the back wall to
emphasise this aspect. As I indicate, I want the action to
be dimly reflected in the windows. In this way, the
audience is constantly presented with two 'realities'
mirroring each other.

Juanita: In a way, Yelena herself suggests this duality. When
I watched Marthinus Basson's mesmerising production I
was struck by the fact that Yelena was presented as being
both vain, amusing, touchingly Chekhovian and a
luckless victim who seemed to be marked by some
almost devilish power from which there was no escape.

Reza: That is precisely how I want her to be portrayed.

Juanita: *On the Lake*, your last play in this series, departs
from naturalism and seems closer to the magic realism
of your earlier plays. I found this unexpected and
refreshing and would like you to tell me why.

Reza: *The Seagull* has completely entranced me for years.
And then I played Nina once and it was a very powerful
experience. What most particularly fascinated me was
the image of the lake which suggests both surface and
depth. For me, the lake reflects this layered play's
metadramatic interaction with theatre forms. As you
know, the play opens on a 'stage within a stage' where a
Symbolist play is about to be performed. Most of the
characters make fun of the play but the performance has
far reaching consequences and the almost ghostly little
stage is still mentioned in the final Act. Also, of course,
both Madame Arkadina and Nina are actresses and
Chekhov uses – which is most unusual for that time –
Hamlet as an intertext. And, so, it always seemed to me
that Chekhov is sensing the presence of other theatre
forms 'waiting' under the surface of naturalism.

Juanita: Was Chekhov interested in new theatre forms?

Reza: Well, he had a profound admiration for
Maeterlinck's other-worldly symbolist plays. He was also
appalled at the detailed naturalism of Stanislavsky's

productions of his plays. He felt a strong kinship with actor-director Meyerhold, who revolutionised Russian theatre in the 1920s and -30s.

Juanita: What is *On the Lake* about?

Reza: The action of the play revolves around Konstantin's symbolist play which is once again about to be staged. But the action and characters are filtered through the prism of Nina's dream-state and so the style of the play is really magic-comic. I suppose one could say that it presents the Chekhovian world as seen through a distorting fairground mirror.

Juanita: I wouldn't use the word 'distorting'. 'Transforming' might be better. After all Nina, as the presiding consciousness, is able to transmute her painful past into a meaningful aesthetic form.

Reza: Yes. That would also mean that in my play she has to free herself from the constraints of naturalism since her character in Chekhov's *The Seagull* is linked to that genre.

Juanita: I certainly feel that the play seems to be releasing a new energy, opening a new door. One last question. Do you think Chekhov would have approved of these 'experiments?'

Reza: From what I've read of Chekhov, he was, among other things, mischievous, childlike and extremely curious. Personally I feel he would have been appalled at the solemn way in which his plays are regarded.
I believe, that if, by entering into the spirit of his work, his plays can provide the impulse for experimentation and 'play', he would have approved. At least I hope so!

Grahamstown, South Africa
2001

THREE SISTERS TWO

to dearest Cheryl and June

Characters

The Prozorovs:

OLGA
fifty, the eldest sister. An old maid. Tall and thin

MASHA
forty-five, the second youngest sister. Once married to
Koolyeegin, now the mistress of Marovsky, a General in the
Red Army. She has a fragile sensuality

IRENA
forty, the youngest sister. An old maid.
Thin and pale. She is somewhat childish

ANDREY
forty-seven, their brother. Balding with a paunch

NATASHA
forty, his wife. Fat and ugly

SOFJA
eighteen, daughter of Andrey and Natasha

Other Characters:

VERSHININ
sixty-two, a wounded General of the White Army
and Masha's lover seventeen years ago. He is tall
and lean and has a wooden leg

IGOR
thirty, a fugitive and a dramatist. Thin and pale

ANFISA
ninety-seven, old Nanny of the Prozorov children

Three Sisters Two was first performed at the Nico Malan Theatre in Cape Town on 16 April 1997 and was produced by The Cape Performing Arts Board, with the following cast:

OLGA, Wilna Snyman

MASHA, Alletta Bezuidenhout

IRENA, Mary Dreyer

ANDREY, Neels Coetzee

NATASHA, Karen van der Laag

SOFJA, Siobhan Hodgson

VERSHININ, Johan Malherbe

IGOR, André Stoltz

ANFISA, Mary Dreyer (snr)

Director, Marthinus Basson

It was first performed in Britain at The Orange Tree Theatre, Richmond on 27 February 2002, with the following cast:

OLGA, Anna Carteret

MASHA, Belinda Lang

IRENA, Kim Thomson

ANDREY, Colin Hurley

NATASHA, Maggie Wells

SOFJA, Octavia Walters

VERSHININ, Jeffry Wickham

IGOR, Timothy Watson

ANFISA, Helen Blatch

Director, Auriol Smith

Setting

The old nursery on the first floor of the Prozorov's house. The house is next to a river in a small town south of Moscow. The nursery wall is covered with faded, floral wallpaper. Pictures on the walls depict scenes from fairy-tales and there is a thread-bare flowered carpet on the floor. The window at the back looks out over the garden and the river. Right front is the passage door which leads to the rest of the house. In the back wall right is the bedroom door. The kitchen door is left front. Centre right, there is a sofa. Just right of the sofa there is a wicker-chair and, left of the sofa, an armchair. Centre left is a table with chairs. Left, next to the kitchen door there is a small child's chair. Against the wall right there is a toy cupboard, and in the corner, back left, there is a narrow child's bed. There is a wicker chair in front of the window. A mirror hangs between the passage door and the toy cupboard.

Period

The summer of 1920. Russia has been in the power of the Bolsheviks since October 1917 but the White Army is still offering resistance.

ACT ONE

Late morning. It is such a blindingly bright day that the nursery seems rather dingy and forgotten. A beam of light shines through the open passage door. ANFISA is sitting on a chair at the open window. She is wearing a white nightdress and a linen nightcap. She is sitting slightly in profile. ANDREY is sitting in the wicker chair. He is sleeping with his mouth open. He is wearing a dirty shirt, crumpled trousers and braces. As the lights go up ANFISA is seen watching him suspiciously over her shoulder.

A few gunshots are heard some distance away.

ANDREY: (*Wakes up. Closes his mouth abruptly.*) What's the time? (*Looking about and seeing ANFISA.*) Where is everybody? (*Mumbles.*) Must be stupid to ask her anything. To go and fall asleep like this... (*Takes out his pocket watch.*) The thing has stopped. If it hadn't been Papa's, I would have flung it against the wall. It's completely bloody useless!

ANFISA: (*Looking at ANDREY.*) Who are you?

ANDREY: (*Sighs.*) Andrey! (*He puts the watch close to his ear.*)

ANFISA: Who?

ANDREY: Andrey Prozorov. (*He swears under his breath and shakes the watch.*)

ANFISA: No you're not! You're not Andrey Prozorov. He's my sweet little boy and you're a very ugly old man.

ANDREY: There it goes again...but who knows for how long. (*Gets up, goes to the door and listens.*) Well, she's not here yet that is for certain. I feel so dizzy... got up too quickly. (*Sits down again.*)

NATASHA: (*Calling off.*) Andrey! Andrey!

ANFISA: I'm nobody's fool!

ANDREY: For god's sake be quiet Nana. Bloody useless! (*Puts the watch back in his pocket.*)
(*NATASHA enters hurriedly from the passage. She is dressed up.*)

NATASHA: Oh here you are. Why didn't you answer me? And just look at you. Stubble and a filthy shirt. It's disgusting.

ANDREY: Leave me alone.

ANFISA: Where is my herring? My pickled herring?

NATASHA: What's this old thing still doing here?

ANDREY: (*Talking to himself,*) I don't feel very well. Dizzy and my ears are humming.

ANFISA: My herring! (*Whining.*) My herring!

NATASHA: What a madhouse. (*Knocks loudly on the bedroom door.*) Irena, you must get rid of the old woman. I've told you before. Your sister will be here at any moment. (*Bangs on the door with the flat of her hand.*) And don't pretend that you can't hear me! (*Mutters angrily.*) Any moment...any moment now. (*Looks at herself in the mirror.*) Dressed in the latest Moscow fashions I suppose and look at me. This dress is almost three years old. As it is she doesn't think much of my taste. Yes! You all think you're better than me!

ANDREY: (*Moans.*) Not again. Not again.

NATASHA: And don't start nagging your sister. You mustn't start all that again. It's her life and she can do what she likes.

(*ANDREY starts whistling tunelessly.*)

General Marovsky can do a lot for our Bobik. And stop trying to irritate me. Think of your son's future in the Red Army and forget about yourself for once.

ANDREY: For once! For once! How dare you say that! It's is all I've ever done! Sacrificed myself for everyone! You! My sisters! The children! Imagine what I could have done... I could have translated hundreds of books... I could have been a professor in Moscow!

NATASHA: (*Sarcastic little laugh.*) Always the same old story!

ANDREY: It is not a bloody story! I could have been someone. Because of you I've worked my fingers to the bone. Wasted my life in this ridiculous place. The Town Council...and now the endless committees! (*Holds his head.*) Oh god... I'm going mad! Mad!

NATASHA: If I have told you once, I've told you a hundred times, you silly little man. Go and get dressed!

(*IGOR appears in the passage door. He is dressed like a very simple peasant.*)

(*Coquettish. Her French accent is atrocious.*) *Bonsoir* monsieur.

IGOR: Madame. (*Kisses her hand.*) You're a vision.

NATASHA: And where have you been all day? (*Little laugh.*) One could almost imagine that you've been avoiding me.

IGOR: (*Sits on the sofa.*) It's just that I have been writing. Writing night and day. What an agony. What an ecstasy.

ANDREY: Get away from me.

NATASHA: You'll have to excuse me. *Mon dieu.* I still have so many little things to do before my sister-in-law arrives. She'll be so happy to meet a famous writer like you. See you later. *Eh bien.*

(*NATASHA exits hurriedly to the passage.*)

ANDREY: I told you to sit further away. You smell of lavender.

IGOR: I'm extremely sorry, Andrey Sergeyevich. (*Goes and sits on the small child's chair against the side wall.*)

ANDREY: I hate the smell of lavender. Old Anfisa (*Indicates.*) used to sprinkle it on our pillows when we were ill. Makes me think of cold-shivers and phlegm.

IGOR: I'm very sorry Andrey Sergeyevich, but you know there isn't any soap. And I'm sure it can't be as bad as the smell of rotten fish. Personally I find the smell of old fish quite revolting.

ANDREY: Fish, fish, why the hell are you talking about fish? (*Puts his palm on his chest.*) Now I've gone and upset myself. It's not good for me but the woman makes me so angry. If you could just hear my heart beating...

IGOR: (*Waving his hand in front of his face. Almost tearful.*) These flies...these flies...these dreadful flies.

(*The sound of shots being fired some way off.*)

Just listen to that. More executions. I can't bear it any more...

ANDREY: (*Taking an old newspaper out of his pocket.*) Maybe someone's shooting partridges. (*Unfolds the newspaper carefully.*)

IGOR: I'm a complete nervous wreck. My stomach is always in a knot. My palms sweaty. And I can't get a decent night's sleep because I am always scared that they'll come and search the house again. It was so terrible... I'll never forget it. Do you know how someone feels who never sleeps, Andrey Sergeyevich? Do you? They feel as if they're drifting...as if they're half asleep and having endless nightmares and that they'll never wake up again.

NATASHA: (*Calling off.*) Olga! Olga!

ANDREY: Just listen to that. I can't bear to hear her voice. (*Folding up the newspaper and putting it in his pocket.*) Is that really the girl I married? I'm asking you? I can hardly believe it...

IGOR: My dear good Andrey Sergeyevich, there's something I have to ask you...

ANDREY: I dreamt about her all that summer... I thought she was the prettiest...the sweetest... I called her 'my dove'... I kissed her eyes. I'm sorry to say this but she's not a human being any more. There's something almost...bestial about her. It's horrible. Horrible.

IGOR: As I was saying...

ANDREY: For instance it makes me feel quite sick to watch her eating. To watch the fat dripping down her three chins and to hear her smacking her lips. And my God, can she snore! She snores like a wild-boar! No. She's not the same person any more, that's all I know. Strange how such things can happen. Such...terrible things. (*Takes the newspaper out of his pocket again.*)

IGOR: What I was trying to say Andrey Sergeyevich...it's really very difficult for me to ask, because I have my pride... (*Passionately. Getting up from his chair.*) But I'm Igor Illich after all! And I have to write with a scratchy nib and watered down ink!

ANDREY: Why are you getting so excited man? I don't understand a word you're saying.

IGOR: It's just so difficult for me... I don't have two roubles to rub together you see. All I want is an exercise book! It's terrible but I have to write on the stinking paper that you buy your fish in every day.

ANDREY: Fish! You seem to have fish on the brain! What's the matter with you. Can't you see I'm trying to read?

IGOR: I know everything is very expensive. But just one or two roubles...

ANDREY: Are you mad? My wife takes the pittance the Party pays me. Says I'll gamble it all away, can you imagine. Can't even buy strings for my violin. Even if I could. But there aren't any.

IGOR: (*Brokenly. Head in hands.*) I'm desperate.

ANDREY: (*Reading.*) Now here's something...

(*OLGA appears in the passage door. There is a basket over her arms and she is carrying a dusty parasol. She is wearing a dark dress with a high collar.*)

OLGA: Just look at me. Covered in dust. I had to stand in that queue for hours. The peasants were shoving and pushing. And the way they smell! I have a terrible headache. (*Throws the parasol onto the chair.*) And after all that I got hardly anything for our coupons. Only soup bones and green potatoes. Today they didn't even have any rotten fish or horse-meat.

(*NATASHA enters briskly. She is carrying a fly-swatter. IGOR makes a little bow.*)

NATASHA: (*To IGOR.*) *Bonsiour* monsieur. (*To OLGA.*) There you are at last. (*Peers into the basket.*) Really, is that all you've got? And what are we going to give your sister?

OLGA: I had to take what they gave me! (*Collapses onto the sofa with the basket on her lap.*) I can't any more... I simply can't. I'm in a state of collapse. Every day in that endless queue...in the heat...among all those dirty people.

(*IRENA opens the bedroom door. She looks half asleep and is carrying a small basket. Her light dress is crumpled.*)

NATASHA: About time! And look at all the lines and folds on your cheek. That comes from sleeping too much. (*She swats the flies on the windowsill and sweeps them onto the floor with the side of the fly-swatter.*)

OLGA: And since my glasses broke, I can hardly see where I'm going. Today I fell down twice. It makes me feel so awful.

(*NATASHA vigorously and repeatedly swats the flies on the table.*)

I heard someone behind me saying 'There goes our
former headmistress. And look at her now. Completely
drunk.' (*Slightly tearful.*) Can you imagine?

NATASHA: (*Sweeping the flies onto the floor.*) Irena, I want
you to take the old woman out before your sister arrives.

IRENA: But Masha will be so glad to see Nana Anfisa.

NATASHA: I really don't see why we've had to put up with
that old woman for all these years. (*Closes the window.*)

ANDREY: Why are you closing the window? It's so hot in
here.

IRENA: She doesn't have anyone else.

NATASHA: There are too many flies at this time of the
day. And the horrible smell of the Onegin's garbage.
What will Masha say?

IRENA: (*Rubbing her cheek.*) I'm just going out for a while to
pick some roses for Masha. To put them next to her bed.
(*Exits through the passage door.*)

OLGA: (*Calling after her.*) Why don't you put your hat on?
(*NATASHA takes the basket from OLGA and exits to the
kitchen.*)

IGOR: (*Following her.*) Madame... There is something that
I'd like to talk to you about... (*Exits after her.*)

OLGA: I don't have to tell you how much Masha's letter
upset me. Since I read it I've felt simply dreadful. But
that's

as much as I'll say... I won't say any more. (*Sighs.*)
I suppose I should go and get dressed. I don't want
Masha to see me like this. After all these years.
(*Pause.*)
But I'm too tired. I can't even move. (*Puts her palm over
her eyes.*) Five years. Nearly six...
(*NATASHA's high-pitched laugh can be heard from the
kitchen.*)
(*Looks at the bedroom door.*) It's like yesterday. I can still
see poor Koolyghin standing in the bedroom door. Now
why was I here? Surely I was living at the school?
I suppose it was the summer vacation...no, it can't have
been... In any case...he stood there weeping loudly very
early in the morning. Irena and I had such a fright. We'd

been fast asleep you see. 'My Masha has run of with
Marovsky. My Masha has run of with Marovsky.' He
kept saying that over and over again. Poor Koolyghin.
Such a good man.

ANDREY: Man was a fool.

OLGA: You didn't know him as I did. Masha always said
I should have married him. (*Sighs.*) Oh well...no one will
ever know. But we never expected him to do what he did.

ANDREY: (*Reads from the newspaper.*) 'Sixty-three people
froze to death in a cattle-truck on the way to Yaroslavl'.
That's something for you.

OLGA: But for goodness' sake, it's summer. Why are you
always reading from that useless old paper?

ANDREY: And where do you expect me to find another
one? Tell me that? Where will I find a newspaper in this
town?

OLGA: Oh do as you like.
(*NATASHA enters from the kitchen. She moves towards the
bedroom brandishing the fly-swatter.*)

IGOR: (*Following her.*) My dear Madame... I thank you with
all my heart. I will dedicate my play to you.

NATASHA: (*Coquettishly.*) You mustn't forget now. (*Sees
OLGA's umbrella.*) And how can you throw this dusty
thing on the chair? (*To IGOR.*) You'll have to promise me.
(*Exits to bedroom.*)

IGOR: (*Hovering in the bedroom door.*) I'm so very grateful...
(*Sound of vigorous swotting from the bedroom.*)
And there's no hurry. Tomorrow will be soon enough.
(*Becomes aware of OLGA and ANDREY watching him. Looks
sheepish and exits quickly to the passage.
Sound of swotting continues.*)

NATASHA: (*Calls from the bedroom.*) I'm really getting
worried! Where are they? They should have been here
by now!
(*Sound of the bedroom window being shut.*)

ANDREY: (*To OLGA.*) I don't trust him as far as I can throw
him.

OLGA: Well I suppose I should get dressed.
(*Short silence. Sound of a child crying somewhere downstairs.*)

It's starting again. And once it starts it never stops. To think that those kind of people should be living in papa's study. Should use his books for fuel.

(*The crying gets a little louder.*)

It's enough to drive you mad! (*Presses her palms against her temples and screws up her eyes.*)

(*NATASHA enters briskly from the bedroom.*)

NATASHA: Haven't I told you to get dressed? (*Listens.*) That's a real brat. Always bawling. Sofoshka and Bobik were such good children. When Bobik cried I always said 'Who's little boy is crying? Is it maman's little boy?' And then...' (*Pouts her lips and makes small kissing sounds.*) I would kiss him all over his face...

(*OLGA groans.*)

...and he would stop crying. (*Clicks her fingers.*) Just like that.

(*OLGA gets up. She takes the parasol and exits to the bedroom.*) And now Bobik and Sofoshka are all grown up. It's hard to believe. And our Bobik is goodness knows where in the Red Army.

(*OLGA slams the bedroom door behind her.*) Where are they? They should be here by now. Put away that stupid newspaper and go and dress! (*Puts the fly-swatter on the windowsill.*)

(*ANDREY sighs. Gets up and fold his newspaper as he moves to the passage door.*) You might as well go and call our General Vershinin. Masha will want to see him. I suppose he's passed out somewhere.

ANDREY: (*Turns at the door.*) And how can you talk like that about Vershinin? You don't understand anything about him.

NATASHA: He is a drunkard and a leech. I understand that much!

ANDREY: 'Passed out'. 'Leech'. Why do you use vulgar words like that! Why do you use them? It's so repulsive! (*IRENA enters breathlessly. There are a few roses in her basket.*)

IRENA: I'm just going to put the roses in some water. Look Andrey... I found some white roses. (*Exits to the kitchen.*)

(*NATASHA gasps with admiration when she notices IGOR standing in the passage door. He is wearing a somewhat crumpled white linen suit.*)

NATASHA: Oh, *tres elegante.*

IGOR: I decided to take off my disguise for the occasion. I don't want your sister to think that Igor Illich is a country bumpkin. (*Laughs.*)

(*ANDREY sits down again and opens his newspaper.*)

NATASHA: *Charmante.*

IGOR: Madame. (*Kisses her hand.*)

ANDREY: (*Reading.*) A professor hanged himself from a pear tree in Smolensk...

IGOR: (*Alarmed.*) Many professors are hanging themselves these days.

NATASHA: Don't pay any attention to him. He only does it to irritate me. But I'm really getting worried now.

IGOR: About what Madame?

NATASHA: About Masha and Sofochka. To think that Sofochka had to ride in the wagon with that brute. (*To ANDREY.*) And why didn't you go with her? What kind of a father are you?

ANDREY: But it's bright daylight. What can possibly happen to her?

NATASHA: You know what these people are like. Always drinking and swearing, with dirt under their fingernails! I should never, ever...

(*OLGA wrenches open the bedroom door.*)

OLGA: She's here! I can hear their voices in the driveway! Irena! Irena! Come here quickly! Masha's arrived!

NATASHA: What a blessing.

(*IRENA comes running out of the kitchen and goes to the bedroom.*)

NATASHA: (*Looking in the mirror.*) And just look at you Andrey? And aren't you ashamed of yourself?

OLGA: I was just busy taking off my dress... You'll have to help me fasten it up again.

IRENA: Yes... Yes. (*Starting to do up OLGA's dress.*)

NATASHA: Look at my hair. (*She surreptitiously sniffs under her arms.*)

OLGA: Quickly now. Don't fumble.

ANDREY: I really don't feel well today. Not well at all.

IRENA: (*Takes OLGA's hand in hers.*) Be good to her Olga. Just don't start preaching again.

OLGA: I'm suddenly so nervous. I'm trembling.

IRENA: So am I. Will she still be our Masha? Will she?

NATASHA: (*To ANDREY.*) And why are you just sitting there?

(*NATASHA and IRENA embrace hurriedly and exit through the passage door.*)

IRENA: (*Off.*) Hold my arm.

NATASHA: Aren't you going to come and welcome your sister?

ANDREY: I don't feel very well. I think I'll stay here.

NATASHA: How can you be so rude!

(*IGOR sprinkles lavender on his hands.*)

ANDREY: (*Suddenly very agitated.*) What am I supposed to do? I don't know what to say to her! You know how I feel. You know how I feel about everything. (*Gets up and moves about in agitation.*) Her life in Moscow with the swine Marovsky...

NATASHA: (*Hissing.*) Be quiet! Do you want her to hear?

ANDREY: It's no use trying to pretend... It's dreadful. It's scandalous. I can only be glad that Mama is not here to see it.

NATASHA: There you go again. You'll spoil everything! (*Exits hurriedly.*)

ANDREY: (*Suddenly seeing IGOR.*) Don't pretend to look so innocent. I'm sure you know all about my sister's scandalous affairs. I'm sure my dear wife told you everything, the gossip! And I suppose she said that it all started with Vershinin. I know she always blames him.

IGOR: I assure you, my dear Andrey Sergeyevich...

ANDREY: I'm not your dear Andrey Sergeyevich!

SOFJA: (*Putting her head around the door.*) Pappa, Aunt Masha is here. She's looking wonderful. (*Disappears again.*)

ANDREY: (*Muttering.*) I'm so anxious. I can hardly breathe. What will she think of us? She'll see everything with new eyes. She might even despise us. Still living the same ridiculous lives. (*Becoming aware of IGOR again.*) If anyone is to blame, it's Koolygin. She should never have married that damned fool. And I suppose she told you about this too. (*Puts his two fingers against his temple.*) Bang!
(*IGOR looks completely bewildered.*
MASHA appears in the passage door. She is wearing a dark dress and a small stylish hat with a short veil. She seems pale and exhausted.)

MASHA: (*Quietly.*) Andrusha...
(*ANDREY looks up and sees her. He is overcome with emotion.*)
Andrusha. (*Slowly walking towards him. Standing in front of him.*) My dearest Andrusha... I've missed you so much.

ANDREY: (*Deeply moved.*) Mashenka. (*Embraces her.*)

MASHA: (*Looking at him.*) Just look at you...you've grown so old. (*Cries and rests her forehead against his chest.*)
(*NATASHA bustles in.*)

NATASHA: I'm so sorry you had to be fetched by that smelly peasant. A real scoundrel. Four roubles for our own horse and our own carriage. It belongs to him now, can you imagine. But one can only keep one's mouth shut. That's all one can do...
(*IRENA enters hurriedly. She is carrying a small elegant suitcase.*)

IRENA: I'll go and put it in your room. Come and see Mashenka. You're sleeping in your old bed. (*Exits to bedroom.*)

MASHA: (*Seeing ANFISA.*) My dearest Nana. I didn't think you'd still be alive. (*Kisses her on the cheek.*) I'm so glad to see you.

ANFISA: (*Grabbing her hand.*) Baryana. Baryana. You're back. Now everything is right again.

MASHA: (*Pulls away.*) She thinks I'm Mamma.

ANDREY: You look a lot like Mamma now. When you stood in the door I had quite a fright.

ANFISA: Baryana. Baryana. (*Cries with joy.*)

NATASHA: (*Calling.*) Come on Irena! Old Anfisa must go
and rest! (*To MASHA.*) And Andrey is a Specialist
Advisor now in the Executive Committee. But I suppose
you know that.

(*OLGA appears in the passage door.*)

MASHA: (*Moving about.*) The old nursery... It seems
different and yet the same.

OLGA: (*Takes MASHA's arm.*) Many things have changed
here. We just have to get used to it. Nana's old room
(*Indicating.*) is the kitchen now. Of course it's horribly
cramped. (*Taking MASHA aside.*) I'm very sorry but
I haven't said anything. Really, I don't know how you
could expect me to. It would be too much for me. You'll
have to do it. Since I got your letter I've been having the
most dreadful headaches.

(*IRENA enters and helps ANFISA up.*)

MASHA: Please. Not now. I just need to rest a little. I'm
sure I'll find the right time...

ANFISA: Are we going now?

IRENA: Yes Nana. (*Leads ANFISA towards the kitchen.*)

NATASHA: And let me introduce you to Igor Illich, the
dramatist. But I hardly need to tell you that. You must
be very surprised to find a famous writer here among
ordinary people like us. (*Little laugh.*)

IGOR: Charmed. (*Small bow.*)

NATASHA: I found him in the summerhouse fast asleep.
He's been walking all the way from Moscow. Can you
imagine that? Such an important man.

IGOR: It was my good fortune.

MASHA: I'm terribly sorry... I didn't quite catch your name.

NATASHA: (*Outraged.*) But surely you've heard of him!

IGOR: (*Coldly.*) Excuse me. I must go and write my fourth
act. (*Exits to passage.*)

NATASHA: (*Calling after him.*) He's writing an important
play about the revolution! But no one is allowed to see it!

ANFISA: (*Shuffling towards the kitchen.*) But I haven't had
my herring. My pickled herring.

IRENA: There you are Nana. We're almost there.

MASHA: (*Looking out of the window.*) Just look...

OLGA: What is it?

(*IRENA and ANFISA exit to the kitchen.*)

MASHA: The...garden.

OLGA: I know. Just look at it.

MASHA: In Moscow I used to dream about the garden...
the tangled flowers...the sweet roses...

OLGA: I know. I know.

NATASHA: There's no one to look after the garden.
Grigori is on the Town Council now. In fact – can you
believe it – he's Deputy-Mayor.

MASHA: Grigori? (*Laughs.*) Our Grigori?

OLGA: Yes. (*Laughs.*) And terribly important. Hardly greets
me when he sees me.

NATASHA: And of course the Onegin's horrible mongrel
digs up all the flowerbeds.

MASHA: Onegins? Who are they?

OLGA: Those people who are living downstairs. But
I remember writing to you.

MASHA: (*Takes off her hat.*) Oh yes...but the post is so bad
these days. (*Puts her hat on the table.*)

NATASHA: (*Touching the hat.*) It's very nice, but I like
something bigger.

(*MASHA tries to open the window.*)

No, *chere* Masha. Please don't. There're are too many flies
at this time of the day. And then that terrible smell.

MASHA: I see. Where are all the birch trees?

NATASHA: They've been chopped down for firewood.

MASHA: Our beautiful, beautiful trees.

NATASHA: Don't upset yourself *cher* Masha. We'll have
some nice tea. I've sent Sofya to ask the Onegin woman
for her samovar. After all, it's a special occasion.

OLGA: Our samovar was confiscated, just imagine.

(*IRENA appears in the kitchen door.*)

IRENA: I can hardly believe that Mashenka is here. It's like
a dream. All I want to do is stand here and look at you.

OLGA: It was actually Irena's samovar, don't you remember?
Uncle Chebutykin gave it to her on her name day...

NATASHA: Where can the child be? I'll have to go and
see. And I'll tell Vershinin that you're here. I'm sure

you'll want to see him after all this time. (*Moves towards the passage door.*)

MASHA: No... Wait a moment... Oh, very well.

(*NATASHA exits to the passage.*)

Yes... I'll never forget the day.

OLGA: It feels like yesterday.

MASHA: (*To IRENA.*) You were wearing a white dress... You looked like an angel... And suddenly...out of the blue... Alexander Vershinin arrived. We didn't know him at all...and to think... (*She leans on the table.*)

OLGA: Come and sit down Masha. You look exhausted.

IRENA: And I'll get you a little water. (*Exits quickly to the kitchen.*)

NATASHA: (*Off. At some distance.*) Sofya! Sofya!

MASHA: (*Sitting down slowly.*) You're so good to me...so good to me. (*Puts her hand in front of her eyes.*)

OLGA: Come on now...you'll make me cry.

(*Short silence.*)

ANDREY: (*Too loudly.*) Well then Masha...it'll amuse you to hear about the Countess Rasenskaya's house. We never liked the old crow. Of course she took to her heels when the trouble started. Some deserters moved in, they cut a hole in the upstairs floor and used the ballroom as a toilet. (*Laughs.*) As a toilet! (*Laughs.*) Serves her right, the old snob.

(*MASHA gives a half-hearted little laugh.*)

IRENA: (*Entering with a glass of water.*) Have a little water Mashenka.

MASHA: Thank you. (*Taking the glass.*) It's really nothing... it's just a journey... It was so awful. I travelled in a cattle truck like an animal.

(*VERSHININ appears in the doorway and stands there uncertainly. He is wearing a crumpled shirt and trousers with braces. He looks rather dishevelled.*)

OLGA: How horrible!

MASHA: Oh well. (*Little laugh.*) It really wasn't that bad.

(*Gives IRENA the glass.*)

VERSHININ: (*Moves closer.*) Masha Andreyevna?

MASHA: (*Gets up slowly.*) Vershinin? Alexander Vershinin?

VERSHININ: So you still know me Masha Andreyevna?
(*He kisses her hand.*) I'm really quite surprised. (*Laughs.*)
I mean, look at me. Old and grey with a wooden leg.

IRENA: Don't talk like that Alexander. (*Takes a few quick
sips from the glass.*)

VERSHININ: It's true isn't it? (*Laugh.*) But Masha
Sergeyevna, you are still as beautiful as ever.

MASHA: Alexander Vershinin... Who could have thought?
(*They look at each other.*)

IRENA: I suppose you heard that they made Alexander a
general? (*She sits.*)

MASHA: Yes, I heard. Congratulations.

VERSHININ: Oh that was long ago. Everything is different
now. The White Army hardly exists any more and I'm an
old man with a dirty collar.
(*Short silence.*)
Well then. Who could have thought? Seventeen years
ago the military band was playing. Such a rousing march
I remember.

MASHA: (*Softly.*) Not just rousing. Triumphant. It was
actually...indecent.

VERSHININ: I was still quite a young man with romantic
dreams. And we were marching to Poland.

MASHA: (*Little laugh.*) And my heart was broken (*Little
laugh.*) Dear, dear Vershinin. (*Moves about restlessly.*) To be
home again... It's so wonderful...the dear old nursery...
(*SOFJA puts her head around the door. She is wearing a
nurse's veil.*)

SOFJA: (*Laughs.*) Mamma is terribly angry. The Onegin
woman said she couldn't have the Samovar and she's
gone to ask next door. I must go to work now. Bye bye.
See you later Aunt Masha. (*Disappears again.*)

MASHA: How she's grown up. And she's so pretty.

ANDREY: She looks like you when you were young.

MASHA: Oh, come now. You make me feel old.

ANDREY: Well none of us are getting any younger, let's
face it.

VERSHININ: Except Masha Sergeyevna.

MASHA: Thank you Vershinin. You've always known how to flatter a woman.
(*Silence.*)

VERSHININ: (*Deeply moved.*) Masha... Masha Andreyevna...seeing you brings back so many memories. (*Short silence.*) Do you remember? (*Starts humming a sweet romantic tune.*) Da de da de dum...de dum de dum de da da da.

MASHA: Yes, now I remember...it brings everything back. (*She looks at him.*) Da de da de dum.

VERSHININ/MASHA: (*Together looking at each other.*) Da de da de dum...de dum de dum de da da da.
(*IRENA leaves abruptly and exits to the kitchen. Short silence.*)

VERSHININ: Well then... I'm sure you ladies have a great deal to talk about. Please excuse me. (*Moves towards the passage door.*)

ANDREY: Wait old friend. I'm coming with you. All these women make me nervous.
(*VERSHININ laughs. ANDREY and VERSHININ exit. Short silence.*)

MASHA: I hardly knew him.

IRENA: (*In the kitchen door.*) He's suffered a lot.

MASHA: Where are his wife and his two daughters?

OLGA: But I wrote about it in a letter. Oh, I forget...the post.

IRENA: They all died in a cholera epidemic.

MASHA: How terrible. (*Short silence.*) He was everything to me...when he left my life seemed so mean and... unimportant...

OLGA: Please Masha. I'd rather not hear about it.

MASHA: (*Looking out of the window.*) I used to cry every night. I used to hide my face in the pillow so that Koolyhegin wouldn't hear me.

OLGA: Yes. (*Sighs.*) Poor Koolyhegin.

MASHA: (*Leans her forehead against the windowpane.*) I know... I know you've always blamed me. Poor Koolyhegin. If I hadn't been such a wicked woman then he wouldn't have shot himself through the head. Was it the head? No one ever bothered to tell me.

OLGA: Masha! Please!

MASHA: (*Turns and looks at OLGA. Speaks in a 'schoolmaster's' voice.*) 'Amo, amas, amat.' 'Five out of ten for good behaviour Masha.' 'Sanguina in herba.' Is that what you really wanted? That I should be a dutiful wife? Night after night...to lie next to him as if I were lying in my grave!

OLGA: I feel quite ill. I can't bear such things. I simply can't! (*Storms out and slams the bedroom door behind her.*) (*Silence. IRENA looks down at her hands.*)

MASHA: (*Moves slowly to the bedroom door. Knocks softly.*) Olga... Olga... Forgive me...please.

OLGA: (*Off.*) Go away.

MASHA: (*Softly.*) You're right...you're right... I'm a bad woman...a useless person.

IRENA: Mashenka...don't talk like that.

MASHA: Everything I do is so completely useless.

IRENA: Mashenka...you're our sister and that's all that matters. Please...come and sit here with me. (*MASHA moves to the sofa and sits down next to IRENA.*)

MASHA: Poor Koolyhegin... He should have married Olga. She would have made him happy. (*Leans back and closes her eyes.*)

IRENA: That's right. Rest for a little while. (*A short silence. Then the sound of a very screechy out-of-tune violin being played somewhere off.*)

MASHA: (*Still with her eyes closed.*) Good God, but that sounds absolutely dreadful. Andrey never used to play that badly.

IRENA: Poor Andrusha. His violin only has two strings left and he doesn't tune them because he's afraid they'll also break.

MASHA: Too horrible. (*She laughs. Short silence. She moves her head from side to side.*) This heat... I'd forgotten how oppressive the heat could be here. Oh well, I'll feel much better after a nice hot bath.

IRENA: I'm so sorry Mashenka...but there aren't any servants to bring up the water. We have to wash in the river now.

MASHA: (*Pulls a face.*) Sometimes I forget... Dearest Irena
would you do me a little favour?

IRENA: Of course. Anything.

MASHA: Won't you please fetch my fan for me. It's right at
the top of the suitcase. I'm suddenly so tired that I can
hardly move.

IRENA: (*Exiting quickly to the bedroom.*) I won't be long.

OLGA: (*Off.*) There's a chink in the curtain. Won't you close
it properly?

IRENA: (*Off.*) Is that better?

(*IRENA enters with the fan.*)

OLGA: (*Off.*) And shut the door!

IRENA: I'm sorry. (*Shuts the door and sits down next to
MASHA.*)

(*MASHA takes the fan and starts fanning herself slowly.*)
I missed you so much. (*Kisses her shoulder.*) You must
never go away again. Never. Promise me.

MASHA: (*Laughs.*) I promise. Oh, I'm quite dizzy from this
heat.

IRENA: You smell so nice.

MASHA: It's patchoulli. Marovsky is very fond of it. He
even puts it on his beard. I always say 'my darling, you
smell more like a sultan than like a general in the Red
Army.' (*Turns her head away.*) I'm sorry, does it make you
uncomfortable if I talk about him?

IRENA: No. Not at all.

(*Silence.*

*IRENA covers her face with her hands and gives a strange
little laugh.*)

MASHA: Why are you laughing?

IRENA: At last...there's someone I can talk to.

MASHA: What about?

IRENA: Mashenka...you've seen Alexander Vershinin...he's
aged a lot...and he's not always quite sober. I know
that... I know. But... I love him. I do. I've waited so long
to tell someone. When he was ill I used to sleep in front
of his door...without anyone knowing...in case he
needed me in the night. I'm blushing. Don't look at me.
I suppose you think I'm foolish.

MASHA: Love is never foolish. And what about him? How does he feel?

IRENA: He's very nice to me. But then he's nice to everybody. Maybe he doesn't want to say anything because he thinks he's too old. Or maybe he thinks... that I'm too plain. (*Lifts her face to MASHA.*) Look at me. I've lost my looks. I'm so pale and there are black rings under my eyes.

MASHA: All I can see is my dearest Irena. (*Kisses IRENA on the forehead.*) I suppose... I've also changed.

IRENA: Oh, no. You look just the same.

MASHA: Really? Or are you only saying so? You know you can tell me the truth.

IRENA: It is the truth. I promise.

MASHA: It's because I look after myself. Because I don't just let myself go.
(*IRENA turns her head away.*)
(*Takes IRENA's hand in hers.*) I'll tell you what... I'll question him.

IRENA: But...

MASHA: Don't be worried... I'll do it very carefully.

OLGA: (*Off.*) Irena! Come and rub my temples! I've got a terrible headache.

IRENA: Just a moment!

MASHA: You want to know the truth don't you? It's better isn't it?
(*IRENA hesitates for a moment and then nods.*)
Well then...

IRENA: (*Looks at MASHA.*) Oh, Masha... Masha... I'm afraid. (*Throws her arms around MASHA's neck and presses her head against her shoulder.*)

OLGA: (*Off, after a short silence.*) Irena! Irena!
(*In the silence ANDREY's screeching violin can still be heard. The lights fade to black.*)

End of Act One.

ACT TWO

The same day. Just before sunset. The sky that can be seen through the open window is a dense blue and gradually it softens to smudgy pastels. The set remains unchanged except for a small cigar case and a lighter which are lying on the sofa. VERSHININ is sitting at the table and writing in an exercise book with a stubby pencil. Outside, some distance away, the fierce barking and growling of a dog can be heard. As the action starts, the sound gets louder and is accompanied by the cries of a man in distress. VERSHININ is so absorbed by his writing that he doesn't seem to notice.

VERSHININ: (*Talks as he writes.*) ' 'And you must be Olga, the eldest'. I said. She smiled.' (*Thinks.*) No...no... (*Makes a note.*) 'She nodded. 'And you are Masha. And you must be Irena, the youngest. How big you've all grown...' '
(*The barking and cries of distress stop abruptly.*)
(*Takes a penknife out of his pocket and starts sharpening his pencil.*) Strange... I can't remember so well any more...
(*IGOR stumbles through the passage door. He is clutching his leg and groaning.*)

IGOR: That brute bit me! That mongrel! Oh my God, I only hope that it hasn't broken the skin. (*Falls onto the sofa.*) Don't just sit there Alexander Ignatevich! Come and help me.

VERSHININ: What am I supposed to do?

IGOR: Come and look! I can't stand the sight of blood! (*Pulls up his trousers-leg.*)

VERSHININ: (*Getting up slowly.*) He's just a bit over friendly the poor animal. He only bites if someone runs away.

IGOR: Of course I ran away! What do you expect?

VERSHININ: But why?

IGOR: (*Groaning with pain.*) I saw a man down at the river. I should never have taken off my disguise. One of those men wearing dark glasses. One of those terrible comrades. Can you see? Is it very bad?

VERSHININ: (*Examines IGOR's leg.*) It's red, but I can't see any blood.

IGOR: Look very carefully. (*Groans.*) When I looked again he disappeared. Now he'll tell them where I am. Ouch! You're hurting me!

VERSHININ: I'm sorry. The skin isn't broken. You're very lucky. A fellow in my regiment got bitten by a dog and he died the most terrible death. And don't distress yourself. Maybe the man was just fishing. (*Goes to the table and sits down again.*)

IGOR: Fishing! You should have seen him! A face like death itself. (*Starts breathing strangely.*) They're afraid of me...because I write the truth. And now they're coming for me... I know it. They're coming for me... (*He starts retching. He clamps his hand over his mouth and rushes to the kitchen.*)

(*The sound of someone vomiting loudly in the kitchen. VERSHININ starts sharpening his pencil again.*)

(*In the kitchen door. Wiping his mouth with the back of his hand.*) I'm sorry but I don't have a handkerchief.

VERSHININ: And what did the ladies think when you ran away like a scared rabbit? (*Laughs.*)

IGOR: There's nothing to laugh about. If they find you here it'll be all up with you General Vershinin of the White Army.

VERSHININ: (*Quietly.*) I know. (*Laughs.*) I hope Sofja didn't see you. (*Mimicking IGOR.*) 'Sofja... Sofja...in you there is the silence...the silence of daffodils.' (*Laughs.*)

IGOR: Disgusting to eavesdrop like that. (*Short silence.*) In any case... I'm too far removed from trivialities like falling in love!

VERSHININ: She's such a lovely girl. So full of life.

IGOR: Oh just be quiet.

VERSHININ: She reminds me of Masha when she was young. When I first knew her. Yes, my friend...love is the greatest adventure.

IGOR: Old letcher! I think you have an eye on her yourself!

NATASHA: (*Off.*) Igor! Igor!

VERSHININ: You're a stupid man. You're a very stupid man!

IGOR: (*Outraged.*) Excuse me! Do you know who you're talking to?

(*NATASHA rushes into the room.*)

NATASHA: Mon cher, what's wrong? One moment you were there and the next moment you were gone.

VERSHININ: The Onegin's mongrel bit him. (*Closing his exercise book and getting up.*) Well I think I'll also go down to the river. Maybe I'll catch a comrade or two. (*Exits whistling a happy tune.*)

NATASHA: I never know what that man is talking about. Do you know what the Onegin woman told me? She saw him herself. Selling his old war-medals for drink. Oh, mon cher, did that horrible dog really bite you?

IGOR: It's nothing. Don't concern yourself Madame.

NATASHA: But you're so pale and covered in perspiration. (*Wipes his forehead with her lace handkerchief. He pulls away.*) You poor thing... I'll go and get you some water. (*Exits to the kitchen.*)

IGOR: (*Calling after her.*) No! I don't want any!

NATASHA: (*Calls from the kitchen.*) I'll ask Sofja for some iodine when she gets back. How disgusting! Ugh! The old woman puked in the drinking water!

IGOR: I'm really not thirsty!

NATASHA: Too disgusting. (*Entering.*) We have to get rid of that old thing! Oh mon cher, show me where.

IGOR: It's nothing.

NATASHA: (*Teasing.*) You don't have to be so brave.

(*IGOR points to his calf.*

NATASHA goes down on her knees in front of him and lifts his trouser-leg.)

IGOR: Be careful. It hurts.

NATASHA: It's very bruised.

IGOR: At least it hasn't broken the skin. That's the important thing.

NATASHA: They would have a dog like that. (*Looks up at him. Puts her hands on his knees. Softly.*) Igor... Igor Ignatevich...when I'm close to you... I...can't you feel me trembling...and my heart is beating so fast...

IGOR: Madame, please...

NATASHA: No, don't say anything. I know you feel the same. I've known all this time. The way you look at me...

IGOR: Madame...

NATASHA: (*Breathless little laugh. Gets up quickly.*) I'm blushing like a young girl. Don't look at me. I know I'm a married woman and you have such high principles, but... (*Laughs breathlessly.*) I just can't help myself... (*Laughs.*) And Andrey... I can assure you...he really wouldn't mind at all.

IGOR: (*Getting up.*) I'm really touched Madame...

NATASHA: Not Madame. Call me Natasha. Say it.

IGOR: (*Reluctantly.*) Natasha.

NATASHA: Oh...say it again.

IGOR: Natasha.

NATASHA: Oh... It makes me tingle all over.
(*She suddenly rushes at him and embraces him passionately.*)

IGOR: (*Pushing her away.*) The fact is...this is not a good time.

NATASHA: What do you mean?

IGOR: I was seen this afternoon down at the river by a Bolshevik spy. A special agent. Now my life is in danger. They'll be coming for me. And that's why I have to flee...my dear Natasha.

NATASHA: Poor darling. But I'll hide you. I'll hide you in the cellar. No one needs to know.

IGOR: I have friends in the South. That would be the best. All I need is a little money for a train ticket.

NATASHA: Please don't go. No one else talks to me. No one needs me. You said it yourself. That I have an artistic soul. You're the only one who understands me.

IGOR: I know dear Natasha...it really breaks my heart. But I have to leave.

NATASHA: I can't bear it. Please. (*Throws her arms around him.*)

IGOR: (*Pushes her away.*) I have to go... I have to. But if I could only borrow a few roubles for a ticket...that would really save my life.

NATASHA: 'A few roubles.' So that's how it is. Always 'just a few roubles.' I'm such a fool... (*Cries and presses her hand against her mouth.*)

IGOR: But dearest Natasha...

NATASHA: I'm not your dearest Natasha! And you're not a gentleman! You're...you're the lowest form of life! If I think how you've been following me about. Always looking at me so sheepishly. You won't get anything out of me again! Just go! Go! Get out of my sight!
(*The voices of ANDREY and MASHA can be heard on the stairs.*)

NATASHA: (*Hissing.*) You're a disgusting leech. (*Rushes into the kitchen.*)
(*MASHA and ANDREY enter. ANDREY is breathless and MASHA is holding his arm. MASHA is wearing a sun-hat.*)

OLGA: (*Off.*) Just like that! Out of the blue!
(*OLGA enters. She is carrying a parasol.*)
Two quite decent men. Or that's what I thought. (*Snorts.*)

ANDREY: I'm exhausted. I think my heart is going to stop. (*Sits in the wicker chair.*)

MASHA: And I'm not even breathless.

IGOR: Excuse me... (*He exits limping through the passage door.*)

OLGA: Said they were the inspectors of the New Educational System. I even gave them tea. (*Throws her parasol onto the table.*) And then I had to hear how everything was going to change. We wouldn't even be allowed to sing our anthem. We had to sing 'Free Poland'. Imagine. (*Sits down.*)
(*MASHA takes her hat off and goes into the bedroom.*)
(*Calling after her.*) And do you know what they did then! They went into the hall and took down the portraits of the Czar and the Czarina. And in their place they put up portraits of those two horrible men! You know who I mean. With their small, wicked eyes. (*Seems overcome.*)

MASHA: (*Entering. Looks at herself in the mirror and touches her hair.*) Poor Olga. (*She hums the romantic tune that she and VERSHININ were humming in Act One.*)
(*ANDREY unfolds his newspaper.*)

NATASHA: (*Storming in tearful.*) That old woman puked in the drinking water. You must get rid of her! I won't have her in this house another day!

ANDREY: (*Reading loudly.*) 'Hundreds die of dysentery in Moscow.'

NATASHA: Haven't I told you! I'm sick and tired of the stupid old newspaper!! (*Grabs the newspaper and tears it up. Storms out into the passage.*)

ANDREY: (*Bewildered. Picking up the pieces.*) There you have it...

MASHA: (*Bursts out laughing.*) She hasn't changed. (*Pushes up her sleeve and inspects her arm.*)

OLGA: And just after they left I took them down. And the next morning we sang our anthem as usual. A week later I got a letter... 'Your services are no longer required.' Not even 'We're sorry to inform you...' but 'your services are no longer required.'

MASHA: Poor Olga. Believe me, it could have been worse. Just look at my arms. Covered in mosquito bites. I'd forgotten about the mosquitoes down at the river.

OLGA: You have to work...or else you feel so lost.

MASHA: Huge bites. I have such a delicate skin. It takes days for the marks to go away. (*She goes to the window and leans out.*)

OLGA: Oh well... (*Gets up slowly.*)

MASHA: There's Irena now. (*Waving.*) Halloo!
(*IRENA's 'halloo' can be heard faintly from outside.*)

OLGA: (*Standing behind her and looking out.*) And how do you find her?

MASHA: She's seems very pale.

OLGA: And her eyes are so deep in their sockets. At night she often gets a fever...

ANDREY: We're not a strong family. Mamma and Pappa died quite early. And I don't have much time left either.

MASHA: (*Teasing. Going to him and kissing him on top of his head.*) Poor Andrusha. And what's wrong with you?

OLGA: She won't see a doctor. I've tried. She says there's nothing wrong with her.

ANDREY: I can't even name all my complaints. The list is far too long. But my heart is the worst.

OLGA: (*Calling out of the window.*) Come inside now! There's dew on the grass!

ANDREY: Come and feel. Feel. (*Takes MASHA's hand and presses it against his chest.*) Can you feel how it flutters. It hardly beats at all.

MASHA: But I can't feel anything. Help Olga! Poor Andrusha has died without noticing. (*Laughs.*)

OLGA: Don't be so silly.

MASHA: (*Going back to the window.*) I actually had a fright when I saw her. She's so terribly pale.

ANDREY: (*Looking at the passage door.*) Shhht!

OLGA: (*Whispering.*) And sometimes it seems as if she's in another world.

IRENA: (*Entering. There is a basket over her arm and she is wearing a straw hat.*) I got so many. (*Goes towards the kitchen.*) They're still growing in all the old places. (*Calls from the kitchen.*) I was so happy! So happy to see your face at the window Mashenka! (*Enters without the basket or the straw hat.*) It was like a dream. A dream. Here we all are…together again. Come now Andrusha, be glad. Why must you always have such a long face? Oh, I feel so… I feel… (*Laughs breathlessly.*)

OLGA: Come and sit Irena.

IRENA: I feel as if we've been playing in the garden and if Nana Anfisa has just called us in to have our supper.

MASHA: And Pappa will be coming up to see us. Looking so handsome in his uniform.

(*A peaceful silence. MASHA lies on the sofa.*)

(*Stretching her arms above her head.*) Now I feel as if I'm really here. I'm here.

(*Silence. ANDREY wipes his eyes on his sleeve. Suddenly the sound of a heavy church bell falling resoundingly to the ground and landing with a booming thud.*)

What on earth was that?

OLGA: It was a church bell falling.

MASHA: A church bell?

OLGA: Yes. You know how many old churches there are in the town…well every now and then they need a church

bell to melt down for ammunition. Then they chop it
loose and it falls to the ground.

IRENA: We've grown used to it...to the bells falling.

MASHA: I always loved to listen to the bells...ringing for
the evening service.

IRENA: There are still a few.

ANDREY: It's a ridiculous business. Ridiculous.

(*Silence. MASHA yawns.*)

OLGA: Don't you put your hand in front of your mouth
when you yawn? You live so 'grandly' in Moscow and
you still don't have any manners.

(*VERSHININ knocks on the open passage door.*)

ANDREY: Come in my dear fellow. Come in. I've just been
saying how ridiculous it is. The church bells that keep
falling.

VERSHININ: I've just come to fetch my book. Sorry to
interrupt. (*Moves towards the table.*)

ANDREY: No come and sit down Alexander Ignatevich.
I need your support. As you can see I'm surrounded by
women.

IRENA: Yes come and sit down Alexander. (*Gets up and
takes his arm.*) I picked some mushrooms down at the
river. I know how much you like them.

VERSHININ: You're right, dear Irena.

ANDREY: Natasha tore up my newspaper! Flew at me and
tore it up. I don't know what could have possessed her.
Have you ever heard of anything like that?

IRENA: I'm going to cook them for you myself. Just the
way you like them.

VERSHININ: (*Sitting at the table.*) You're so good to me
Irena Sergeyevna.

ANDREY: I wish we had a pack of cards. We could have
played a few hands of poker. Just imagine that.

IRENA: Alexander is much too busy for things like that,
Andrusha. He's always busy writing. (*She leans on the
table.*) You never want to tell us what you're writing
about. Come now Alexander...tell us. Please.

VERSHININ: You're much too curious Irena Sergeyevna.

(*IRENA laughs girlishly.*)

MASHA: Come on. Tell us Vershinin. What are you writing?

VERSHININ: (*Shy laugh.*) My memoirs. (*Laughs.*) Everyone knows about it. And I'm sure you laugh at me behind my back. Who wants to read anything about an insignificant fellow like me?

IRENA: It's not true Alexander. (*Sits at the table.*)

VERSHININ: About an insignificant life like mine.

MASHA: (*Stretches her arms above her head.*) I'm sure it's very shocking. Sensational. Come. Read to us. Amuse us.

ANDREY: Yes, come on old fellow. I don't have a newspaper any more. You're our only hope.

IRENA: He doesn't want to. You can see he doesn't want to.

MASHA: He's shy that's all. (*Coquettish laugh.*) You really don't need to be shy with us. We know each other much too well for that.

VERSHININ: (*Looks at MASHA. Smiles.*) Yes... I suppose you're right.

IRENA: (*Quickly.*) If you don't want to Alexander, we'll forgive you.

ANDREY: Nonsense! You must read to us immediately. (*Talks to himself.*) I'm terribly thirsty but the old woman has vomited in the water.

VERSHININ: Very well then.

(*MASHA and IRENA applaud.*)

(*Embarrassed.*) I write things down...because everything passes so quickly... I want to be able to say... 'There it is. There's my life'. (*Laughs.*) But so much of it has slipped away. Years and faces...simply vanished. But then things come back, and I think 'yes...yes...that's it! I've got it'. And sometimes the dead seem to be looking at me and they say 'Tell them about us. We want them to know...'

ANDREY: Come on old fellow. Stop talking and start reading. I like stories. Mamma used to read us a fairytale every night.

MASHA: (*Lighting a small cigar.*) But I only want to hear what you've written about us. If you've written about us. Or are we too unimportant?

OLGA: Horrible smelly cigar. It makes me feel quite ill.

MASHA: It's such a small one. And the window is open.

OLGA: It gives me a headache. Really, you've picked up such bad habits.

IRENA: Come now Olga.

VERSHININ: (*Laughs.*) Well as it so happens I wrote about you this afternoon.

MASHA: Well then, read it to us.

VERSHININ: I was describing how I met you.

IRENA: (*Teasing.*) Shame on you Alexander. See how much you've written already and you're only getting to us now.

ANDREY: (*Laugh.*) Yes we think we're so important and we're only a postscript in your memoirs. Now that's something for you.

VERSHININ: It's not true. You know how much you all mean to me. More than I can ever say.
(*Short silence.*)

MASHA: Read now. I want to hear what you've written about us.
(*VERSHININ clears his throat and pages through the exercise book.*)
Silence ladies and gentlemen. The performance will begin.

VERSHININ: (*Reminiscing.*) Yes...the first time I met all of you...

IRENA: It was on my Name day.

VERSHININ: Yes. I was forty-three. Still quite a young man. (*Starts reading very formally.*) 'One morning I put on my best uniform because I'd decided to go and introduce myself to the late Colonel Prozorov's daughters.'

ANDREY: And what about his son? That's how it's always been. Everybody forgets about me.

IRENA: Be quiet Andrusha. Please go on Alexander.

VERSHININ: (*Reading.*) 'Although so many years had passed I still thought of them as small girls. I was extremely surprised when I met them and saw that they'd changed into young women.' (*Lifts his head.*) I don't know...the time that passes so quickly... I simply can't understand it...

ANDREY: Who can my dear fellow...who can.

VERSHININ: The sun was shining... I forgot to mention that...but I remember it now. Bright sunshine.

OLGA: It was the first day of sunshine after a long winter.

VERSHININ: 'Of course I cannot...'

OLGA: (*Interrupting him.*) It was almost exactly a year after father's funeral...but on the day of his funeral it snowed... rained and snowed...

MASHA: Shhht.

VERSHININ: (*Continues.*) I said, 'Of course I cannot remember you so well, but I knew your father. The excellent Colonel Prozorov.

OLGA: That's odd. I can't remember anything about that. (*Short silence.*)

VERSHININ: (*Lifts his head and looks at them.*) Little did I know that that day would be the start of some of the happiest times of my life.

ANDREY: (*Moved.*) I suppose it's better not to know too much.

MASHA: (*Puts out her cigar.*) You must write everything about us Vershinin. You must immortalise us.

ANDREY: I remember that day very well. I was young... not unattractive...and look at me now! Old and sickly. And repulsive.

IRENA: Don't say that Andrusha! It's not true.

ANDREY: I know it is! Repulsive. Repulsive. I know it! (*Gets up and starts walking about restlessly.*) I was young and I was in love. I was on top of the world. Filled with hope. I would go to Moscow and become a professor. Everyone thought so. Moscow! An important man. I would translate the world's literature into our tender language. So many dreams...everything ahead of you... and then it's all in the past. When does it happen...when is it suddenly too late?
(*Short silence. His face convulses with pain and he bangs on the table with the flat of his hand.*)
And now...even when I try I can't translate anything. When I put the words down on paper they look like nothing. When I get to the end of a sentence I've forgotten how the sentence begins. Sometimes...

I forget the simplest word. (*Starts crying.*) What is left for me? Sickness...old age...endless committees! And no one can do anything for me! No one can help me! It's unbearable! O god, I don't want to live like this any more. I don't want to! I'm going to get my revolver. One clean shot straight through the head! (*Storms out into the passage.*)

MASHA: You don't really think he'll...

OLGA: No, no. He always talks like this. In any case we've hidden his revolver.

IRENA: Look. (*Gets up.*) Under the mattress. (*Takes the revolver out from under the children's bed's mattress.*)

OLGA: Put back that thing.
(*IRENA hides the revolver under the mattress again.*)
If the Bolsheviks find it here, we'll be in big trouble.

IRENA: Sofja hid it here. (*Looks in the toy cupboard.*) And just imagine where she hid the bullets.

OLGA: Why is Sofja so late tonight? In the evenings the streets are really not safe.

VERSHININ: (*Turns his head away.*) She's a good child.

IRENA: (*To MASHA.*) The hospital is in the Protopopovs old house.
(*IRENA finds a jack-in-the-box in the toy cupboard.*)
In here. (*She opens the box and the jack-in-the-box jumps out.*)
(*They all laugh.*)

MASHA: Go on Vershinin. We also want to remember everything again.

OLGA: We were so excited to meet someone from Moscow. Then we still believed that we'd go back some day. Yes, that's all we dreamt about.

IRENA: 'Moscow... Moscow... Moscow...'

OLGA: 'Yes! As soon as possible!' (*Little laugh.*) That was twenty years ago. Well I suppose that's how it goes.
(*NATASHA enters.*)

NATASHA: (*Very friendly to MASHA.*) I'm so sorry I lost my temper dear Masha...but sometimes things become too much for me. In any case I have a nice surprise for you.

I just ran into Nina Zarechnaya. The famous actress. The darling of the new Regime.

MASHA: I know of her. But what is she doing here?

NATASHA: The Party has given her the best rooms in the house. The ballroom and the dining room just underneath us. When she wants to get away from Moscow then she comes here to have a rest. She comes about once a month. Each time with another man. They say theatre people are like that. In any case, what I wanted to say, is that she's invited us all to her party tonight. She's going back to Moscow tomorrow.

OLGA: Even if I don't like mixing with those kind of people, I wouldn't mind having a decent meal for a change.

VERSHININ: You can say that again! (*To MASHA.*) For a while we caught wonderful fresh fish in the fishpond, but then the Onegin woman drowned her kittens in it.

MASHA: I'm afraid I won't be able to go.

NATASHA: But that's why she invited us. She was most impressed. She said she met you once with General Marovski.

MASHA: But how did she know that I was here?

NATASHA: I told her of course.

MASHA: (*In despair.*) And why did you go and tell her! I don't want anyone to know!

NATASHA: Excuse me. You seem to think you're so important!

MASHA: You could never keep your mouth shut! You've always been a terrible gossip! (*Presses her hands against her temples.*) I feel as if I'm going out of my mind!

NATASHA: Who do you think you are talking to me like this? How dare you! You're just a kept woman! That's all you are!

OLGA: (*Getting up.*) Always pretending to be better than we are! I don't think you should be so holier than thou! As if we'll ever forget about Protopopov! As if poor Andrey will ever forget about Protopopov.

VERSHININ: (*Getting up.*) Please!

OLGA: Keep out of this! It has nothing to do with you!
(*VERSHININ sits down again.*)

NATASHA: How dare you say such things! How dare you!
I don't know what you're talking about! (*Storms out to the
passage. In almost immediately.*) And I told you the old
woman puked in the drinking water! Tomorrow I'm
kicking her out! I'm telling you that! This is my house!
And you mustn't forget that!! (*Exits to the passage.*)
(*Short silence. OLGA sits down again.*)

MASHA: (*Talks to herself.*) It's too late now. She knows I'm
here. I might as well go along tonight.

OLGA: Vershinin, I want to apologise. I shouldn't have
spoken to you like that. These days we always seem to
be quarrelling about the slightest thing. It's because
everything is so uncertain. We're living on the edge of a
precipice. We don't know what's waiting for us and we
have to live from day to day.

VERSHININ: Yes. That's true. (*Gets up. Goes to the window
and looks out.*)

MASHA: It's intolerable.

IRENA: I think I must go and fetch fresh water. Poor Nana.
(*Exits to the kitchen.*)

OLGA: (*Gets up and moves to MASHA. Softly.*) Now that
Zarechnaya woman is here, I suppose it makes things
much worse.

MASHA: We don't have much time. I thought that we could
wait for a day or two, but now we'll have to go as soon
as possible

OLGA: How soon?

MASHA: Tomorrow. Tomorrow on the early train.

OLGA: Tomorrow morning. It makes me feel quite ill.

IRENA: (*Entering with the bucket.*) Nana is sleeping just as
I left her. It couldn't have been her.

OLGA: Come on...the bucket is too heavy for you. (*Takes
the bucket from IRENA.*) Let me carry it.

IRENA: Thank you Olga. (*Claps her hands.*) I know! Masha
wanted to go and have a bath. While we're down there
we might as well wash in the river.

OLGA: That's not a bad idea. I really feel very grimy.

IRENA: Masha, will you come?

MASHA: I'll follow you a little later. (*Lies on the sofa.*) Let me just rest for a minute. It's been a long day...

(*OLGA puts down the bucket and goes to the bedroom.*)

IRENA: But you must Mashenka. The river is so dark and still now. Don't you remember? It's like drifting in clouds and upside down trees.

MASHA: Yes, I remember...

OLGA: (*Entering with a white linen cloth over her arm.*) If we want to go we must go now.

IRENA: Promise you will Mashenka.

MASHA: I promise. In a little while.

IRENA: Remember we're waiting for you.

(*OLGA picks up the bucket and OLGA and IRENA exit.*)

(*Off.*) Just walk very very slowly.

(*MASHA closes her eyes.*)

VERSHININ: (*Moves towards the door.*) Well then...

MASHA: Stay here...please. Won't you just stay for a while. You don't have to pay any attention to me... I just don't want to be alone.

VERSHININ: Very well. (*Goes and sits at the table and opens his exercise book.*)

(*Silence. MASHA leans her head on her arm.*)

MASHA: I feel as if my head will burst...it's unbearable... unbearable... I feel as if I'm going mad...

VERSHININ: Dear Masha...what's wrong? Are you unhappy?

MASHA: Yes. I don't think...I've ever been happy. You know I never loved poor Koolyeeghin... You leaving... And then Marovsky... He was unfaithful to me from the start.

VERSHININ: I'm sorry.

MASHA: I was so miserable. I wanted to leave...but I couldn't. You know how these things are... But then one night he came home very late and rather drunk. He kicked off his shoes and fell asleep on the bed. I suddenly saw how small his feet were. Quite ridiculously small. And to make it worse, he was wearing striped socks. It's odd but after that it all seemed to be much more bearable. (*Laughs, then falls silent.*) It's much worse than that. It affects all of us. Even you, my dear.

VERSHININ: What's happened? Tell me!

MASHA: (*Goes to the window and leans out.*) No...I don't want to talk about it. I can't talk about it now. (*Gives a cry of distress.*)

VERSHININ: What's wrong?

MASHA: There's something caught in my hair. Please come and see!

(*VERSHININ gets up and goes to MASHA.*)

MASHA: (*With tightly closed eyes.*) What is it?

VERSHININ: Only a small beetle. (*Catches it and lets it go.*) There. It's flown away.

MASHA: Thank you.

(*Short silence.*)

VERSHININ: But how terrible can it be?

MASHA: This house... (*Looks around.*) This world... their whole world...everything...

VERSHININ: You must tell me.

IRENA: (*Calling from outside.*) Masha! Masha!

MASHA: (*Leans out of the window.*) I'm coming!

VERSHININ: I really have to know, Mashenka.

MASHA: Later... later... I have to find the right time. Oh well... I won't worry about that now. I have to go, they're waiting for me. (*Short silence. Still leaning out of the window, with her back to VERSHININ.*) When you went away...I was so afraid I'd never see you again. When I asked, you said, 'Only time will tell.' It was so sweet with you. Who knows what would have happened if you'd never left.

VERSHININ: Yes. Who knows.

(*IGOR appears in the door.*)

IGOR: Excuse me, but have you seen Natasha Ivanovna? I can't find her anywhere.

VERSHININ: I haven't seen her.

(*MASHA exits. A single church bell starts ringing for the evening service.*)

IGOR: (*Mumbles.*) Thank you. (*Wanders off.*)

(*VERSHININ starts writing again. The church bell continues to ring. SOFJA enters after a while. She is dressed in the white uniform of a nurse.*)

VERSHININ: (*Looking up.*) Sofja. I didn't see you.

SOFJA: A young soldier died tonight. I didn't even know his name...he held my hand so tightly as if he wanted me to go with him.

VERSHININ: Sofoshka...you're much too young...too tender for such things.

SOFJA: No, uncle Alexander, I'm not. No one is. On my way here... I wondered if he was part of everything now...the clouds...the trees...of me.

VERSHININ: I really can't say, my Sofoshka.

SOFJA: (*Sad little laugh.*) But dear uncle Alexander... I thought you knew everything.

VERSHININ: No. Not everything.

SOFJA: When I walked past the church square, there was a meeting. Everyone was arguing and shouting. (*Laughs.*) You should have heard them. And then suddenly it was as if I could hear how everything...every tree...every house...every stone...everything that had to keep quiet for so long...could suddenly speak. And then I thought, 'Yes, it's been worth it after all'.

VERSHININ: Maybe you're right.

IGOR: (*Appearing in the door again.*) I heard your voice, Sofja Andreyevna. Do you know where your mother is? I have to talk to her.

SOFJA: I haven't seen her yet.

VERSHININ: I told you she's not here.

IGOR: Oh well... (*Wanders off.*)

SOFJA: It's become so dark in here. Let me light you a candle. (*Lights a candle and puts it on the table. She sits at the table.*) What are you always writing uncle Alexander? (*The church bell stops ringing.*)

VERSHININ: You can read it one day if you want to. I'm writing about my life. My poor miserable life. (*Laughs.*)

SOFJA: Yes. I want to read it. (*Looks around.*) And to think...

that Bobik and I used to play here every evening when we were small. Bobik had a magic lantern and we used to watch picture-stories on the wall. And now Bobik is somewhere in the Red Army...like the young soldier.

VERSHININ: Don't think about that Sofoshka. (*He puts his hand on hers.*)

SOFJA: Dear uncle Alexander...you're so good to me.
(*Short silence.*)
And where's aunt Masha?

VERSHININ: You aunts have gone down to bathe in the river.

SOFJA: I want to go too. (*Gets up.*) I'll go and give them a fright. They'll think I'm a ghost in my white clothes.
(*She laughs and exits quickly to the passage.*
VERSHININ gets up slowly and goes to the window.)

VERSHININ: (*Looking out.*) There she is... Sofja... Sofoshka...my darling.
(*The light fade to black.*)

End of Act Two.

ACT THREE

Later that evening. A single candle is burning low in the candelabra on the table. A light can be seen under the bedroom door and a broad band of light falls through the open passage door. Tinny dance music played on a gramophone can be heard from the ballroom below. IGOR is standing at the open window. He is still wearing his white linen suit. SOFJA is sitting on the sofa. She is wearing a sweetly girlish evening dress.

SOFJA: (*Busily taking off her shoes.*) Even uncle Alexander is dancing. With his wooden leg. (*Laughs. Takes off her shoes and rubs her toes.*) He's just been dancing with me. He stepped on all my poor toes. (*Laughs.*) Aunt Masha dances so beautifully. I wish you could have seen her. Even aunt Irena is dancing.
(*Silence. SOFJA listens.*)
Just listen to the music...so sweet...

IGOR: That's not music. I think a gramophone is extremely vulgar.

SOFJA: The music breaks my heart. This is such a beautiful night...a night for being in love.

IGOR: If you'd only allowed me, I could have taught you about love. (*Looks at her. Soft and passionate.*)
'How can you look at the Neva?
How can you walk across the bridges?
Since I've been dreaming about you,
All the people tell me I look sad.
The wings of black angels are sharp
and the blood red signal fires
flower like roses in the snow.'

SOFJA: Not again! (*Sighs.*) I've heard it so many times. In any case I know about love. Promise me you'll tell no one...promise me...but I'm in love.

IGOR: (*Upset.*) I think you've had too much to drink. I think you're a little drunk. I don't want you to tell me about your private affairs.

SOFJA: He's a wonderful man. He has sensitive, healing hands...his eyes are deep and dark...when he looks at me...when he talks to me...his voice is soft and warm.

IGOR: Is he anyone I know?

(*The music stops.*)

SOFJA: The young doctor at the hospital. Misha. Oh what a beautiful name. Misha...Misha.

IGOR: Has anything happened between the two of you?

SOFJA: I'm sure he feels the same... I know he does. But he has a wife and a child somewhere.

IGOR: Poor Sofja, you're playing with fire. How can you be so stupid?

SOFJA: I don't care! I want to live! Live! I'd much rather be like aunt Masha than like poor aunt Olga. It's pathetic. Just look at her. Nothing has ever happened to her.

IGOR: I know much more about life than you do and I'm telling you you're playing with fire!

(*The bedroom door opens and OLGA peers through.*)

OLGA: I've a headache. Please don't talk so loudly. (*Closes the door.*)

SOFJA: (*Softly.*) I didn't know she was there. I hope she didn't hear what I said. Do you think she heard?

IGOR: What does it matter? It's the truth isn't it?

SOFJA: I feel so dreadful. I hope she didn't hear me.

(*A sweet waltz is played on the gramophone.*)

(*Putting on her shoes.*) Come and dance with me Igor. I want to dance and dance and never stop.

IGOR: You're being ridiculous. You're quite childish tonight.

(*SOFJA laughs.*)

And what's so funny?

SOFJA: Nothing.

IRENA: (*Appearing breathlessly in the passage door. She wears a frilly evening dress that seems too young for her.*) I'm completely exhausted. (*Falls into the chair.*) I danced too much. (*Breathy little laugh.*) Alexander Vershinin danced with me. (*Coughs.*) I feel so dizzy... Maybe I'm a little drunk. (*Little laugh.*) I've always been very fond of champagne.

IGOR: It's disgusting. We're dying of hunger and they drink champagne!

ANDREY/VERSHININ (*Off. Singing loudly and out of tune.*)
'Love is a red red rose... Love is a fragrant flower...'
(*ANDREY and VERSHININ appear in the passage door.
Both are dressed in evening suits. ANDREY has his arm
around VERSHININ's shoulder. They are both rather drunk.*)

VERSHININ: Ladies and gentlemen... I have something for
you. (*Takes four candles out of the left pocket of his jacket.*)

IRENA: (*Clapping her hands together.*) Candles!

SOFJA: (*Teasing.*) You didn't steal them did you uncle
Alexander?

VERSHININ: But of course! Blew them out and put them
in my pocket!

IRENA: (*Little laugh.*) Oh, Alexander. You're impossible.

VERSHININ: (*Moves to the table and attempts to push the
candles into the candelabra.*) Let there be light!

IRENA: (*Little laugh.*) Wait I'll help you Alexander. (*Gets up
and goes to the table.*)

ANDREY: What an excellent fellow you are Vershinin!
Excellent!

VERSHININ: That's not all! (*Puts his hand in his other pocket,
takes out a bottle of vodka and holds it up.*) Abracadabra!

ANDREY: Vodka! Have you ever!

IRENA: Oh Alexander. (*Little laugh. Lights the candles in the
candelabra.*)

ANDREY: (*Banging on the table.*) Glasses! Immediately!
(*SOFJA laughs and goes to the kitchen.*)
I'll say it again! You're an excellent fellow! (*To IGOR.*)
And you should have seen him dancing with his wooden
leg! (*Laughs.*) That was something to see! (*Waltzes with
one stiff leg.*) Dum de dum de dum. (*Laughs and falls down
in the chair.*) A game of cards would have been just the
thing. But we don't have any more cards... I think we
exchanged them for something.
(*SOFJA enters with a tray and glasses. She puts them on the
table.*)

IRENA: (*Giggles.*) For radishes. (*Uncontrollable giggle.*)

ANDREY: Radishes. Yes.

IRENA: (*Still giggling.*) I'm sorry...I'm being so silly.

(*Giggles.*) I know! Why don't we play lotto! We haven't played it for a long time.

ANDREY: Yes! A magnificent idea!

(*The gramophone record gets stuck. The same musical phrase is heard over and over again.*)

SOFJA: Can I also play? I like lotto.

IRENA: It must be somewhere here... (*Looks in the toy cupboard.*)

IGOR: Just listen to that! It's unbearable!

IRENA: Wait a minute and I'll find it.

(*The music stops.*)

ANDREY: In summer we played outside on the verandah... there were always moths around the lamp.

IRENA: Here it is. It used to be Mamma's when she was a child. Come on. You must all come and sit around the table!

MASHA: (*Appearing in the passage door. She is wearing a stylish evening dress.*) Oh here you are. Suddenly I was left with only Natasha.

ANDREY: What is she doing, the poor thing? Is she making a spectacle of herself again? Just look! Vershinin blew out the candles and put them in his pocket! And a whole bottle of vodka! What do you thing of that?

MASHA: Bravo Vershinin!

ANDREY: And we're going to play lotto!

IRENA: Wait... I'm going to call Olga. She's very fond of lotto.

(*ANDREY pours vodka into the glasses.*)

MASHA: For me too.

(*IRENA knocks on the bedroom door.*)

ANDREY: I suppose you can also drink something Igor Illich. You're quite grown up now after all. (*Laughs.*)

MASHA: (*Looking in the mirror.*) How pale I am. Pale as a ghost.

IRENA: (*At the door.*) Olga! Olga!

ANDREY: (*To IGOR.*) And you must come and play with us. I want to beat you hollow. (*Sits at the table.*)

OLGA: (*Off.*) What is it?

IRENA: We're going to play lotto. We want you to come and play with us.

OLGA: (*Off.*) I'm tired and I have a headache!

IRENA: Please Olga. Don't be like this.

ANDREY: (*Loudly.*) Come on Olga! We're waiting for you. Even Igor Illich, the famous Igor Illich is going to play, isn't that true?

IGOR: Oh well... (*Sits at the table.*)

SOFJA: Come on aunt Olga! Don't be a spoil sport!

ANDREY: We won't start without you!

OLGA: (*Wrenches open the door. Her eyes are red and her hair is dishevelled.*) You're all being impossible!

ANDREY: (*Big announcement.*) Here is Olga!
(*Applause.*)

OLGA: You're behaving stupidly! Very well then...
(*VERSHININ pulls out a chair for her and she sits at the table.*)

IGOR: Are we playing for anything?

VERSHININ: But of course! We are reckless gamblers!

ANDREY: Quite so!

IGOR: But I don't even have a kopek.

SOFJA: What about dried peas? (*Laughs.*) There's a whole bag of dried peas in the kitchen.

VERSHININ: An inspiration, Sofochka! (*Brings the wicker chair to the table.*)
(*SOFJA laughs and exits to the kitchen. VERSHININ sits down at the table.*)

OLGA: (*Softly to MASHA.*) When we've finished playing we must tell them. I can't take it any longer.

IRENA: (*Calling after SOFJA.*) And bring the small stool for Mashenka!

MASHA: (*Calling.*) No! Leave it! I don't want to play. (*To VERSHININ.*) Tonight I can't sit still. I feel so restless...
(*Takes a sip of vodka.*)
(*SOFJA enters with the peas and gives each player a handful. She sits down.*)

IRENA: Who's going to call out? (*While she deals three cards to each player.*) I'm asking...who's going to call out?

OLGA: Me. As usual.

VERSHININ: And how much shall we bet?

ANDREY: Come on old fellow...be completely reckless!

VERSHININ: Shall we say ten? All of ten peas?

(*Everyone laughs. IRENA throws out a heap of lotto blocks in the middle of the table. IRENA and VERSHININ sit down.*)

OLGA: Are you ready? (*Reading the numbers on the wooden blocks which she takes out of a small velvet bag.*) Seven. Thirteen. Six. (*Putting her hand over her eyes.*) It's not only the headache...it was so dreadful...seeing people like that in our house. It made me feel so peculiar...as if I'm not really here any more...as if I'm a spirit haunting my own house.

IRENA: (*Touching her hand.*) Poor Olya.

MASHA: I know how you feel.

ANDREY: Forget about it. We want to enjoy ourselves. Come on! Call out!

OLGA: I'm sorry. Oh well...twenty-three. Thirty. Eleven.

ANDREY: What did you say? The second one?

OLGA: Thirty.

ANDREY: Aah.

OLGA: Twenty. One. Forty-two...

(*IRENA coughs.*)

(*Leaning across and touching IRENA's forehead.*) Why are your cheeks so red? Are you feverish? You shouldn't have been dancing so much.

IRENA: Oh, leave me Olga.

ANDREY: Come now! Are we playing or aren't we?

OLGA: Eight. Thirty-six. Fifteen.

MASHA: (*At the window.*) It's so dark outside. I can't even see one star...

OLGA: Fifty-three. Twenty-five. Nineteen. Three.

(*Waltz music is heard again. MASHA hums and starts dancing in a wide circle around the table.*)

ANDREY: You'll have to hurry up. Look at Sofja. She's almost finished.

OLGA: Seventy-two. Forty.

ANDREY: (*Rubbing his hands.*) Yes...yes...

OLGA: And that unspeakable woman walking on her hands

and doing somersaults…

IGOR: Typical. I'm glad I didn't have to see that.

OLGA: Stop it Masha! You're making me dizzy.

(*MASHA continues to dance and pays no attention.*)

ANDREY: Come on Olga. I want to win!

OLGA: Seventy-eight. Fifty-six. (*Suddenly screaming loudly.*)
I told you to stop it!

(*Short silence. MASHA stops dancing.*)

And close the window, it's getting chilly.

ANDREY: Come on now!

(*MASHA goes to the window and leans out.*)

OLGA: Fifty-five. Forty-three. Thirty-one. Sixty.

VERSHININ: A little slower please.

ANDREY: (*Laughs.*) You must keep up Alexander
Ignatevich. Don't fall behind whatever you do!

MASHA: I think it's going to rain. I can smell the rain.

OLGA: Sixteen. Fifty-two. Four. Thirty-nine.

ANDREY: There it is! I've won! I've won!

(*Applause.*)

VERSHININ: We must drink on that!

ANDREY: Bring your glasses! Immediately!

(*MASHA brings her empty glass to the table.*)

OLGA: Not for me or Irena. And Sofja is too young.

ANDREY: Top it up, top it up.

MASHA: (*Kisses him on his head.*) You have luck on your
side tonight Andrusha.

ANDREY: Yes…yes… I'm a lucky man.

VERSHININ: Let us drink to Andrey Sergeyevich! A
lucky man!

NATASHA: (*Entering from the passage. She is overdressed.*)
What a terrible noise! I could hear you from down there!
I felt so ashamed. What will the people think of you? Oh
I see…you're getting drunk again. (*Pointing to the vodka.*)
And where did you get that? I suppose it's Vershinin.
And while my innocent child is here! (*To SOFJA.*) Go to
bed immediately!

SOFJA: But mamma…we're playing lotto.

NATASHA: I don't want to tell you again!

ANDREY: Shut up you old bitch! You ridiculous old bitch!

NATASHA: How dare you!! Come on Sofja. When men are drunk they turn into beasts.

(*NATASHA and SOFJA exit to the passage.*)

ANDREY: (*Calling after them.*) I'm a lucky man! A lucky man!

VERSHININ: (*Lifting his glass.*) To Andrey Sergeyevich! A lucky man!

(*The music stops.*)

ANDREY: (*Filling his glass.*) And now we must drink to the good General Vershinin. No, no...the excellent General Vershinin!

VERSHININ: (*Laughs.*) Oh, I'm just an unfortunate fellow. A wounded general. But I suppose it's not the end of the world. There are many that are much worse off.

IGOR: Oh god, I hope he's not going to start with his moralising again.

VERSHININ: For instance I might be feeling a little melancholy tonight. Might think I've had a hard life. All I have to do...is to think of that writer... I forget who... who travelled to Siberia. I only have to remember how he described standing on the banks of the frozen Kama, cold and exhausted while the ice blocks were banging against each other as if – and this is how he described it – 'someone was beating on empty coffins with their fists'.

ANDREY: Yes. I know who it is. It's on the tip of my tongue.

VERSHININ: Then I forget about my own sorrows and I think how lucky I am tonight to be here with you...

ANDREY: Sometimes I think I'm losing my mind.

IGOR: (*Very drunk now. To VERSHININ.*) It makes me sick. (*Staggering out of his chair.*) You talk rubbish! Your facile optimism makes me puke! Look! Open your eyes! Our country is falling apart! It's the end of the world!

ANDREY: Just listen to him.

(*NATASHA appears in the passage door and watches them.*)

IGOR: All we can do... (*Making a wild gesture.*) is to face the truth. That's all that's left. In my new play 'Russia in Twilight' Ivan says 'Look! Look!' (*Jumps on his chair and gestures dramatically.*) 'Don't turn away! don't avert your eyes! Look and see how the light is stifled by the darkness!' (*Closes his eyes. Deeply moved.*) 'How the light is stifled by the darkness.'

MASHA: (*Applauds.*) Bravo! Encore!

ANDREY: Why are you being so melodramatic my friend? Surely this is all a farce?

NATASHA: (*Coming closer.*) Why are you talking so much Igor Illich? You're just wasting time. I thought you had to flee.

(*IGOR staggers. He looks sheepish and gets off the chair.*)

OLGA: What are you talking about Natasha?

NATASHA: Our famous author is going to leave us. *Au revoir.* Isn't that so? *Bon voyage.*

IGOR: It's true... I have to leave...as soon as possible.

IRENA: And why so suddenly Igor Illich?

IGOR: Someone saw me...down by the river. A special agent. A spy. I'm not safe here any more.

NATASHA: Who is going to spy on you, you silly little man? You think you're so important.

IGOR: I am Igor Illich!

NATASHA: My husband has never even heard of you. And he's a very learned man.

IGOR: Learned man! Excuse me.

ANDREY: What do you mean by that?

OLGA: Please Andrey. Just leave it.

NATASHA: You're not welcome here any more. You must go. As soon as possible.

ANDREY: Yes! As soon as possible!

IGOR: I will! As soon as the sun comes up! do you think I want to stay among you any longer? Insignificant, half-witted Bourgeoisie! I just waste my time with people like you! (*Exits rapidly to the passage. Almost immediately puts his head around the door.*) You'll only be remembered because I wrote my opus here! And because you sent me packing without a kopek to my name! Barbarians! (*Disappears.*)

MASHA: Well...at least we'll be remembered. (*Laughs.*)

ANDREY: And so my poor wife... I see you and your admirer had a little tiff.

NATASHA: I don't know what you're talking about?

ANDREY: I must say he was rather amusing. Certainly more amusing that the Chairman of the Town Council...certainly more amusing that Protopopov.

NATASHA: You're starting again! I'm tired of the Protopopov story!

ANDREY: Oh, now it's a story? The whole town knew about it! Mashenka, do you know what happened to Protopopov?

OLGA: Must you talk about it? It was so horrible.

IRENA: Please don't talk about it Andrusha.

MASHA: Tell me. I want to know.

ANDREY: (*Laughs.*) The Bolsheviks shot him, stuffed him in his grand piano and threw him in the river.

NATASHA: Stop it!

ANDREY: Something like that makes this whole ridiculous revolution worthwhile. The poor idiot. (*Laughs.*)

MASHA: (*Laughs. Hums and then starts singing.*)
Poor Protopopov. Poor Protopopov.
Stuffed in his piano.
See how he drifts. See how he drifts.
Moving with the flow.

NATASHA: How can you?

OLGA: Stop it! It's really in bad taste.

MASHA: (*Dancing while she sings.*)
Poor Protopopov. Poor Protopopov.
Stuffed in his piano...
(*NATASHA cries and runs into the passage.*
ANDREY laughs uproariously.)

VERSHININ: (*Laughs.*) Masha, you're impossible. But you've always been naughty.

MASHA: (*Seductively, while she dances.*) Very naughty. But you should know.

IRENA: (*Gets up abruptly.*) I'm packing the lotto away. We won't play any more. (*Tearfully.*) I think you're all drunk. You should be ashamed of yourselves. (*Gathers the lotto cards together.*)

VERSHININ: What's wrong Irena?

OLGA: She's tired. That's all.

IRENA: Oh...it's nothing. (*Puts the blocks in the velvet bag.*)

(*Short silence. She turns her head and looks at VERSHININ.*)
Actually...there is something I would like to say to you
Alexander...

VERSHININ: But of course. Whatever you want to. You
know that.

IRENA: I hope you'll forgive me... I hope I'm not speaking
out of turn...but...you're such a good man...such a
wonderful man...and that's why it's so terrible...it upsets
me so...to see you drinking too much...day after day.

VERSHININ: I thank you dear Irena. You're quite right of
course. Quite right.
(*A loud screech is heard from the kitchen. IRENA runs to the
kitchen door and looks in.*)

IRENA: She's only had a dream. (*Going into the kitchen.*)
Shu, shu, Nana. Ssh, ssh.

MASHA: Poor old Anfisa... I wonder what she can be
dreaming about.
(*The music stops.*)

VERSHININ: (*Talking to himself.*) Quite right.
(*Another cry from the kitchen. MASHA lights a small cigar.*)

MASHA: (*Lying on the sofa.*) Maybe she dreams...wonderful
dreams. Maybe she's much happier than we are...maybe
she's dreaming about love.

OLGA: Please! Not that foul cigar again.

MASHA: (*Hums a romantic tune. She and VERSHININ look
at each other.*) Ta ta ra ra ra...ta ra ra ra ra.

VERSHININ: Ta ta ra ra ra...dum de dum de dum.

OLGA: I can't bear it any longer! (*Rushes to MASHA. Takes
the cigar out of her mouth and throws it out of the window.*)

MASHA: I can't believe it! Did you see what she's just
done? She threw my cigar out of the window. (*Strange
little laugh.*) I can't believe it.

ANDREY: Just like that. Now that's something for you.
(*Turns the vodka bottle upside down.*) Not a single drop.

MASHA: (*To OLGA.*) You make me feel as if I'm ten years
old.

IRENA: (*Entering.*) She's sleeping restfully again. Poor
Nana. (*Takes the lotto game and puts it in the toy cupboard.*)

MASHA: You always decided what we could and could not

do. We were terrified of you, isn't that true Irena?

IRENA: (*While she's putting away the lotto game.*) Don't say such things. (*A doll falls out of the cupboard and she puts it back.*)

ANDREY: Olga has thrown Masha's cigar out of the window! What do you think of that?

MASHA: We could never really be children, because there was always Olga. Olga looking at us with those eyes of hers.

OLGA: You should be grateful. When mamma was so ill, someone had to look after you. Especially you. You were always so wild.

MASHA: 'Wild'. Oh, I see. Is that what you call it? Because I've always wanted to get something out of life, to live fully and intensely, you call me 'wild'. You were never 'wild'. No, no one could accuse you of that. And look at you. The good example. (*Exploding.*) Half blind! Bitter! Dried up!

IRENA: Masha!

ANDREY: What are you saying?

OLGA: (*Quietly.*) How can you talk to me like that? I can't believe it. I simply can't believe it. (*Goes to the bedroom and closes the door behind her.*)

MASHA: (*Crying.*) It's just that I'm so…unhappy…so terribly anxious. I don't know what I'm going to do. I don't know how I can tell you. I feel as if I'm going insane!

IRENA: What's wrong Mashenka?

VERSHININ: (*Getting up.*) Oh well…it's getting late.

MASHA: Please stay here Vershinin. Please… I can't do this alone.

ANDREY: Do what? What is she talking about?

MASHA: I don't know how to begin… I simply don't know…

IRENA: You're frightening me.

MASHA: Well you see… Marovsky (*Little laugh.*) my lover…has been arrested.

ANDREY: I wish you wouldn't call him that. And what has

he done?

MASHA: Nothing! He's done nothing! You know what it's like these days. One day you're important and the next day you're an enemy of the state. (*Quietly.*) Lenin had him arrested. They had...a disagreement.

IRENA: I'm so sorry, Mashenka. No wonder.

ANDREY: But it's shocking! They can't do things like that!

VERSHININ: They can do what they like old friend. Don't you know that yet?

IRENA: Poor Masha.

ANDREY: Olga was right. She said if you came back so suddenly, something must be wrong.

MASHA: Oh, really? Is that what she said?

IRENA: She didn't mean anything by it.

(*Short silence.*)

MASHA: But that's not the worst. I had to flee for my life. And I know you're also in danger.

ANDREY: That's rubbish! We have nothing to do with Marovsky! I don't even like the man.

IRENA: You know it's not true Andrusha. (*To MASHA.*) He doesn't mean it.

ANDREY: I've never liked him.

MASHA: That's the way it is these days. If someone is arrested...it doesn't end there.

ANDREY: Nonsense! I don't have to listen to this.

MASHA: But it's true! That's why I came here! To tell you and to warn you.

ANDREY: I don't want to hear another word about this. It's giving me palpitations.

IRENA: Don't talk like that Masha. You're frightening me.

MASHA: Never mind... I've found somewhere in Moscow where we'll be safe.

IRENA: (*Cries. Very upset.*) What are you saying? That we have to leave? That we have to leave our home?

MASHA: Just for a time.

ANDREY: Don't listen to her. (*Shouting.*) Why did you ever come back? You always cause trouble! Always have!

VERSHININ: Andrey, my friend I think you must listen to

her. Don't be foolish.

ANDREY: Keep out of this! I know what you've been to her! I'm a Specialist Advisor. I'm on all the committees. I'm an important man in this town! The people hold me in high regard! No one would do anything to us! They wouldn't dare!

MASHA: But everything has changed now, can't you understand that. He became a Special Advisor…you were allowed to stay in the house…because of Marovsky. He protected you because I asked him to. I asked him to.

IRENA: And what's going to happen now?

ANDREY: So! You're saying that I'm worthless! You're saying that I'm completely useless without your so-called General Marovsky! How dare you!

MASHA: Think, Andrey. Why else would they keep you? Let's face it, everyone knows how absent-minded and lazy you are.

ANDREY: Absent-minded and lazy! So you dare point a finger at me! It's you! You are nothing without Marovsky! You! Marovsky's whore!

VERSHININ: Come now!

ANDREY: (*Making a fist and swinging wild.*) Keep out of this! I've told you! Shut your mouth you bastard! It's you who started everything! You turned her into an adulterous slut! (*To MASHA.*) I'm ashamed of you. For years I've been ashamed of you! I'm only glad Mamma is dead! Yes, I'm glad! I'm glad that she's been spared this! (*Pointing at MASHA.*) To see what you've become.

MASHA: What do you know about Mamma? If I'm like anybody in this family, I'm like Mamma.

ANDREY: But you're insane! Mamma was refined…an angel…and you're a whore! A whore!

MASHA: And what about uncle Chebutykin?

ANDREY: And what about him? He's been dead for years.

MASHA: Don't you remember how he used to say…over and over again…that he would never marry because he was in love with Mamma?

ANDREY: Good god! That's not to say…

MASHA: Everyone knew! Everyone in the army. I'm sure
  Vershinin knew. Marovsky knows. It was quite a scandal!
IRENA: Stop it! Stop it!
MASHA: (*Beside herself.*) And why do you think he came to
  live with us after Pappa died? And why did he give Irena
  such expensive presents? (*Pointing to IRENA.*) Maybe
  blood is thicker than water!
ANDREY: Shut up you vile bitch! (*Wants to slap MASHA
  But staggers and falls against the table.*) It's not true...it's
  not true...
MASHA: (*Bursting into tears.*) Please...it's not true...
  please...don't believe me...please...oh god...
ANDREY: (*Covering his face with the back of his hand.*) Stay
  away from me! Stay away! (*Staggers out through the passage
  door.*)
IRENA: You've spoilt everything. (*Cries.*)
OLGA: (*Wrenching open the door. She is wearing a nightdress
  and a thin plait hangs over her shoulder.*) What's happening
  in here? Are you all mad? (*To MASHA.*) Since you
  arrived here this morning all hell has broken loose!
IRENA: (*Runs to OLGA.*) Olya... Oh, Olya...
OLGA: My poor little Irena. (*Puts her arms around her. To
  MASHA.*) Just look at her. Completely ashen. Are you
  satisfied now? And don't think we'll go anywhere with
  you. Anything will be better than that.
  (*MASHA turns her head away. OLGA leads IRENA to the
  bedroom. ANDREY's violin is heard. OLGA turns and rushes
  to the passage door.*)
  Stop it!! Stop it!! I detest your disgusting playing!!
  I detest it!!
  (*ANDREY stops playing. OLGA rushes back to the bedroom
  dragging IRENA behind her. She closes the bedroom door.
  Silence. MASHA slowly sits down on the sofa. For a while
  she stares out in front of her.*)
MASHA: (*Softly.*) What have I done? I'm a wicked person.
  I wish I was dead. (*Closes her eyes.*) Dead.
VERSHININ: Don't say that. You don't always think,
  that's all.

(*The sound of gentle rain falling.*)

MASHA: It's like a bad dream...everything is like a bad dream...

VERSHININ: Let them all calm down and then I'll talk to them. I'll explain to them. I'll make them understand, I promise you. Don't upset yourself any more.

MASHA: Thank you, Vershinin. Dear Vershinin.

(*Muffled sound of IRENA weeping in the bedroom.*)

VERSHININ: I think... I'll go and lie down for a while.

MASHA: Please...just for a few moments. Come and sit with me...talk to me...

VERSHININ: (*Sits next to her.*) What do you want me to talk about?

MASHA: Anything...anything...

(*Short silence.*)

Listen...it's raining very softly... Just listen... (*Closes her eyes.*) Sleep...sleep... I wish I could go to sleep and never wake up again. (*Opens her eyes and looks at VERSHININ.*) Do you remember the first time...do you? It was very late...and the wind was howling in the chimney. Then you suddenly looked at me and said 'I love you... I love you... I love you more than life itself'. Do you remember?

VERSHININ: I'm sorry... I don't seem to remember.

MASHA: Oh, Vershinin... I feel so strange. I feel as if my head is drifting above my body. (*Gets up and moves about restlessly.*) Poor Marovsky. I try not even to think about him. About what he must be suffering. If he's still alive. Vershinin... I'll have to lie to them. They still dream about Moscow...but Moscow has changed into a sort of hell. Crime, disease. And everywhere the smell of sewage and death. Our old house in Staraya Basmanyana Street...our lovely old house...has become a brothel for Red Army officers. Did you know that?

VERSHININ: No.

MASHA: We'll have to hide in damp dark rooms. But how can I tell them that? If they know, they'll never come with me. Is it wrong of me not to tell them? Is it? I have jewels

I could sell. Maybe we could escape to Petersburg...then to Archangel...to Oslo...and then to Paris. I've always wanted to see Paris...maybe we could do that...maybe everything isn't as terrible as it seems...
(*Short silence.*)
Just listen to me. Just listen. I talk and talk and I don't even know what I'm saying. It's as if I can't even hear my own voice any more. (*Sits next to VERSHININ.*) But you must come with us of course, my dear.
VERSHININ: I'm a fugitive. I don't have any travel documents.
MASHA: Oh god, what are you going to do?
VERSHININ: Don't worry about me. You've got enough to think about. I'll manage.
MASHA: Yes, I'm sure you will.
(*Silence.*)
There are shadows in the room. I can't even see you very clearly. Oh Vershinin...can't we believe that we're young again...young and in love...that I'm your only love... and that you're mine. Let's pretend that we still adore each other...please...please...and we must believe it...
(*Closes her eyes and throwing her head back.*) Kiss me, Vershinin... (*Touching her throat.*) Kiss me here.
(*VERSHININ looks at MASHA for a moment, then he bends down and kisses her as the light fades to black.*)

End of Act Three.

ACT FOUR

*Early morning the next day. Pale sunlight is reflected on the floor
and the walls. The carpet has been rolled up and there are sheets
over the sofa and chairs. The vodka bottle, the tray and the glasses
have all been taken off and the chairs are in their usual positions.
The candelabra is still on the table as well as VERSHININ's exercise
book and his pencil.*

*OLGA enters through the passage door with a dusty portmanteau.
She is dressed in a severe travelling-costume. She is holding the
portmanteau at some distance from her as she moves towards the
bedroom. When she notices the sheets over the furniture she stops. For
a moment she stands motionless, then she drops the portmanteau with
a thud and pulls off the sheets.*

NATASHA: (*Entering from the passage with a half-full cloth
bag in her one hand. She is wearing a dressing gown, slippers
and curling-papers in her hair.*) But what are you doing?
I've just put the sheets on and you're taking them off
again.

OLGA: You're such a stupid woman! Do you think we're
going away for a little holiday and when we come back
everything will be without dust and exactly the same!

NATASHA: (*Tries to take the sheets from OLGA.*) Give that to
me!

OLGA: There'll be nothing left, do you hear me! Nothing!
The moment we've left they'll descend like vultures! It's
as if I can see it with my own eyes. And soon other
people will be living here. People who know nothing
about us. Nothing about our life... (*Cries and throws the
sheets onto the floor.*)
(*Shots being fired some distance away.*)

NATASHA: (*Picks up the sheets and starts arranging them over
the furniture again.*) What do you know! I've written a
letter to Bobik. He'll do something. They think a lot of
him in the Red Army. He has a great future. Everyone
says so. He'll do something, you'll see!

(*IGOR enters through the passage door. He is staggering under the weight of a heavy suitcase which he is carrying in his arms. He is dressed like a peasant again.*)

OLGA: (*Snorts.*) Bobik! You've always been a silly woman! (*Rushes to the bedroom and slams the door.*)

NATASHA: (*Arranging the sheets over the furniture.*) What are you still doing here?

IGOR: The clasp's broken. I'm looking for something to tie it up with. (*Exits to the kitchen.*)
(*Shots being fired at some distance away.*)

NATASHA: (*Calling after him.*) Too full! That's why the clasp broke! I suppose it's all the stuff you've pinched from us!
(*OLGA jerks open the bedroom door, storms in, grabs the portmanteau, storms out to the bedroom again and slams the door behind her.*)

IGOR: (*Off.*) How can you say that Natasha Ivanovna? (*Entering.*) I'm not a thief!

NATASHA: Open it then! Open it and let me see.

IGOR: Leave it alone! It's mine!

NATASHA: Then I'll have to do it myself. (*Lifts the lid with her foot and tips over the suitcase. The contents fall out.*)

IGOR: Just see what you've done!

NATASHA: Books! Are you completely stupid to carry all these heavy things with you. You can't eat books. Can't even sell them.

IGOR: Please be careful.

NATASHA: What a ridiculous man you are. (*Little laugh.*)
(*Silence. IGOR bends down and starts packing everything back into the suitcase. NATASHA sits heavily on a chair with the cloth bag on her lap.*)
I'm completely finished. I never slept a wink. As usual I have to do everything. Nobody helps me because they're all too hopeless. The Prozorovs. The whole lot of them. I remember my father telling me 'My poor child, you're making a big mistake if you marry a Prozorov. They think they're so high and mighty, but actually they're useless.'

(*Sound of shots being fired some distance away and a muffled explosion.*)

IGOR: I can understand that you're upset...*chere* Natahsa... I really can't blame you in the least.

NATASHA: And where is Andrey? Did he sell the things? Did he get enough money for the tickets? Knowing him, I suppose he fell off the horse. That mangy old nag. And for that I had to give the Onegins my locket. Of course, I took out Bobik's baby hair.

IGOR: (*Ingratiating himself.*) It's a dreadful, dreadful situation for all of us. Like a nightmare. I mean...what's going to happen to us all? (*Closes his eyes. Soft and dramatic.*) 'Slowly...slowly the sun goes down. A blood red womb giving birth to the darkness...'

NATASHA: (*Getting up.*) How disgusting! One doesn't talk about things like that. (*Moves to the table. Takes the candelabra and puts it in the cloth bag.*) I think that's everything. (*Moves towards passage door.*)

IGOR: Wait, Natasha Ivanovna! Wait! We've known such wonderful times together... I'll never forget you... I beg you...have mercy on me! It's crawling with the Bolsheviks today. I'm only asking for a few roubles...

NATASHA: The same old story. 'A few roubles. A few roubles!' (*Puts her hand into the cloth bag and scratches around.*) Well then...sell that and there you have your roubles! (*Throws a silver serviette-ring onto the ground and it rolls away.*)

IGOR: (*Crawling after it.*) Thank you...thank you.

NATASHA: Pathetic. And to think... (*Exits rapidly to the passage.*)

IGOR: (*Picking up the serviette-ring.*) Is it silver plated or is it solid silver? Let me see...let me see...yes. There's the mark. It's silver! It's silver!

OLGA: (*Opens the bedroom door. Squinting into the room.*) Is that you, Andrey?

IGOR: It's me, Olga Sergeyevna. Igor Illich. I'm getting ready to leave.

OLGA: I'm sorry but I don't see very well. Won't you close the passage door. The Onegin woman is spying on us. She can't wait to get her hands on our things.

(*IGOR closes the passage door.*)

What's that shining in your hand?

IGOR: It's something that Natasha Ivanovna gave me. You can ask her yourself.

OLGA: Give it here. Let me see.

IGOR: It's mine! (*Hides the serviette ring behind his back.*) It's just an old serviette ring.

OLGA: I want to see it!

(*IGOR gives the serviette ring to OLGA. He is very unwilling.*)

But just look...it was my mother's serviette ring. Her initials are engraved on it.

IGOR: But now it's mine! Please give it back to me!

OLGA: Just imagine. The woman had no right to give this away. My mother's serviette ring. (*Takes the serviette ring, goes back into the bedroom and slams the door in IGOR's face.*) (*IGOR remains motionless. He looks completely lost.*)

SOFJA: (*Breathlessly entering from the passage. She is wearing a simple dress.*) Has anyone been looking for me? Is pappa back? Have you heard the shots and explosions? They say there are quite a lot of wounded.

IGOR: Yes. The poor White Army. The Bolsheviks are everywhere.

SOFJA: I'm so glad you're alone because I can't tell anyone else. (*Sits on the sofa.*) Why are you standing around like that? Come and sit next to me.

(*IGOR sits next to SOFJA. He looks lost and stares out in front of him.*)

So then I went to the hospital and pretended that I was just going to ask about Nana Anfisa. To ask if they'll fetch her to look after her and they said they would. But of course I was hoping to see him...you can imagine.

IGOR: Who?

SOFJA: The doctor. I told you last night. Don't you remember? Don't tell me you've forgotten! Well... I looked everywhere and once I even thought I heard his voice. I started trembling and my heart was beating wildly. But it wasn't him after all. Then someone told me he was away for the day...that's he's gone to the battlefield. And I was so hoping to see him for the last time...so hoping to look into his eyes and to see that he would miss me...

(*MASHA and IRENA enter from the passage. MASHA is wearing the same dress as in Act One and IRENA is wearing a light coloured travelling-costume.*)

IRENA: I really tried, but he kept looking at the river and he didn't say anything. (*She moves to the window.*)

SOFJA: (*Tearfully.*) Well... I must get ready... (*Exits quickly into the passage.*)

(*IGOR takes off his belt.*)

IRENA: (*Looking through the window.*) And just look at him. He's wearing his White Army general's uniform and his imperial medals. Imagine what will happen if they see him! Imagine what will happen!

MASHA: Leave him for a while and then you can go and tell him I want to speak to him.

IGOR: (*Also looking out of the window.*) The Idiot. He's a danger to all of us!

IRENA: (*To MASHA.*) I told him 'Alexander it's very cold outside. It's damp out here after the rain. And you know the damp makes your leg ache.' And then I told him... it makes me blush to think of it... 'What you need Alexander, is someone to look after you.' (*Little laugh.*) Just imagine...but he didn't understand...just kept looking at the river and saying 'Yes, Irena'.

MASHA: (*Bumping into IGOR's suitcase.*) What is this doing in the middle of the floor?

IGOR: (*Trying to fasten the suitcase with his belt.*) My clasp's broken. But it's too short. (*Gets up.*) I'll have to look for something else. (*Exits to the kitchen.*)

MASHA: (*Taking the sheets off the furniture.*) How revolting! You should only cover a corpse with a sheet. (*Walking about restlessly.*) Where is Andrey all this time? I'm afraid we'll miss the train. (*Yawning.*) I'm so sleepy... I never slept at all. My head feels so heavy and thick... (*Sits on the sofa and rests her head on her arms.*)

IRENA: (*Looking through the window.*) It's so early. It reminds me of the mornings when we used to go to school.

MASHA: Yes...

IRENA: (*Looks at MASHA.*) Mashenka, I'm so afraid. I don't want to go away. This is my home...and I'm afraid...of strange places...and strange people.

MASHA: (*Lifting her head.*) Come here. Come and sit with me.

(*IRENA goes and sits next to MASHA on the sofa. MASHA draws her close and she puts her head on MASHA's shoulder.*) Don't be afraid. You'll see...nothing is ever as bad as we imagined it to be.

(*IGOR enters unnoticed. He is carrying a piece of rope. He bends down next to his suitcase.*)

IRENA: I can hardly remember Moscow at all. I remember how I longed to go back there. But when I think about it...everything started fading away... I can still remember our old house in Basmanyana Street. A few of the rooms. And how it felt. I know mamma was there... but I can't see her any more. No matter how hard I try... I can't see her face any more.

MASHA: (*Stroking IRENA's hair.*) There now...you'll make me cry.

(*ANDREY stumbles in through the passage door and falls into a chair. He is wearing a crumpled linen suit.*)

MASHA: Andrey! Thank god!

IRENA: What's wrong Andrusha? Are you feeling ill? (*Gets up and goes to him.*)

ANDREY: (*Breathlessly.*) Feel my heart. Just feel how it's beating.

(*IRENA goes to him and presses her hand against his chest.*)

IRENA: It's beating very fast. I'll get you a little water. (*Exits quickly to the kitchen.*)

ANDREY: And I'm covered in perspiration. (*He wipes his forehead on his sleeve.*) Being jolted about on that bony old mare. Must the station be so bloody far from town? No one knows why. No-one's ever found out.

IRENA: (*Back with the water.*) Drink a little. But not too fast.

IGOR: (*Getting up and picking up his suitcase.*) I think that should hold.

ANDREY: (*Drinks the water very quickly.*) Thank you. (*Hiccups.*)

IRENA: I told you not to drink too fast, Andrusha.
(*The rope becomes undone and everything falls out of IGOR's
suitcase again.*)

IGOR: Bloody hell!

ANDREY: What's going on? (*Hiccups.*)

IRENA: It's just Igor Illich's suitcase. The clasp broke.

IGOR: I'll have to make double knots. (*Bends down and starts
putting everything back in the suitcase again.*)

IRENA: (*Knocking on the bedroom door.*) Olga! Andrusha is
here!

OLGA: (*Opening the door.*) Thank goodness. (*Seeing the
contents of the suitcase on the floor.*) What a mess!

IGOR: (*Mumbling.*) I'm sorry.

OLGA: Oh, be quiet. (*Rubbings her hand across her forehead.*)
I have the most dreadful headache.

MASHA: Close your eyes and think of a white horse.

ANDREY: Rubbish. (*Hiccups.*) That never works.

IRENA: He drank the water too fast.

ANDREY: All that way on an empty stomach. (*Hiccups.*) I'm
not going back again. I'm staying right here. (*Hiccups.*)

MASHA: (*Goes to ANDREY.*) Come now, Andrusha. (*Puts her
hand on his shoulder.*) We can never manage without you.

ANDREY: (*Sarcastic.*) Oh, and yesterday I was lazy and
absent-minded.

MASHA: Come now…we depend on you. You're the man
of the house. You'll have to look after us, Andrusha.

IRENA: She's right Andrusha.

OLGA: Come on! Tell us! What happened?

ANDREY: Well… I sold my violin… (*Hiccups.*) Well…
I suppose that's the end of it… (*Hiccups.*)

OLGA: And Mamma's rings?
(*ANDREY nods. IRENA bursts into tears. OLGA turns her
head away.*)

IGOR: (*While he is tying a knot.*) And I suppose they cheated
you as well.

OLGA: It has nothing to do with you. (*Screaming.*) Stop
hiccuping Andrey! I can't bear it any longer!
(*ANDREY gets a fright and stops hiccuping.*)
(*Tearfully.*) There you are. (*Sits down.*)

NATASHA: (*Puts her head round the door.*) Did you manage to get the tickets?

ANDREY: Yes I did. I had to pay a fortune. Just look. (*He pulls the linings out of his pockets.*) There's nothing left.

NATASHA: So much for seven tickets! And Moscow isn't even very far!

ANDREY: I suppose you blame me! After everything I had to suffer you still blame me!

NATASHA: I'm only asking! (*Disappears again.*)

ANDREY: It was horrible. You can hardly imagine. So many people: the wounded, old women, children, chickens, goats. Even pigs. The noise was unbearable. And the stench. A real circus. Ba. (*Wiping his forehead with his sleeve.*) All the trains are full because everyone wants to be somewhere else.

IGOR: Typical. As if anywhere else would be better.

ANDREY: Some people have been waiting for days. The more you pay, the easier it is to get a ticket. That's why I had to pay so much. (*To MASHA.*) And all the way I was thinking... 'Why am I doing this? It's madness. We should stay just where we are.'

MASHA: Come now Andrey.

IGOR: Masha Sergeyevna's right. Lenin's Cheka tortures people for days and sometimes even weeks. They flay them alive. They pull their skin off bit-by-bit.

IRENA: (*Clapping her hand in front of her mouth.*) How terrible.

OLGA: Be quiet! You're frightening the child! And what is your problem with that stupid suitcase? (*Gets up.*)

MASHA: Do you have enough tickets?

ANDREY: (*Taking the tickets out of his inner-pocket and counts them.*) Yes. That's right. Six. And I said we all wanted to be together.

(*OLGA moves stealthily to the passage door.*)

IRENA: Six? And what about Alexander?

ANDREY: But he doesn't have any identity documents.

MASHA: I'm sure he'll manage to get to us. You mustn't worry.

IRENA: (*Uncertainly.*) Do you really think so?

MASHA: Of course.

OLGA: (*Storms into the passage. Screaming.*) Get away! Get away, you dreadful woman! (*Enters and closes the door. Breathlessly.*) That Onegin woman has been creeping around here since dawn. It's too horrible. (*Presses her hand to her mouth.*)
(*Short silence.*)

ANDREY: We'll have to travel in a cattle-truck. Compartments are reserved for military personnel. What a mess.

IGOR: Yes. That's the way it is. But what else could you expect?

MASHA: I travelled in a cattle-truck yesterday. It really isn't so bad.

IRENA: Is it very dark in the cattle-truck?

MASHA: Not completely. And by nightfall we'll be in Moscow.

OLGA: Moscow. (*Wry little laugh.*) Imagine that.

ANDREY: The conductor told me we shouldn't take much luggage. There isn't really space for luggage. He said we must take small bundles because they're easier to fit in. And another thing...he said everything is opened and searched. If we have any valuables, we must hide them in our shoes or in our mouths.

OLGA: Dreadful.

ANDREY: Or if it's small enough, you can push it up your nose.

OLGA: That's enough.

ANDREY: It's no use hiding it on your person, because they search you.

IRENA: Oh!

MASHA: They don't always do it.
(*IGOR picks up his suitcase and starts walking about with it.*)

ANDREY: What's the man doing? Is he mad?

IGOR: Yes, that should hold. Oh well... I suppose I'll have to be on my way. (*Doesn't move.*)

MASHA: All the best.

ANDREY: Oh well...goodbye then... (*Doesn't move.*)

OLGA/IRENA: (*Together.*) Goodbye.

IGOR: Farewell.

ANDREY: Yes. Whatever.

IGOR: (*Moves slowly to the passage door where he stops.*) And where am I supposed to go? I'm asking you. I don't even have a kopek. Nothing. You don't know how lucky you are. You have tickets. You can get away. But what about me? I ask you.

(*MASHA exits quickly to the bedroom.*)

Am I supposed to walk all the way to the Black Sea?

MASHA: (*Entering with her handbag.*) Take this. (*Taking a few coins out of her handbag.*) That's all I have. (*Gives the coins to IGOR.*)

IGOR: Thank you. Thank you very much. At least this will help me for part of the way.

OLGA: Masha! We could have used that on the train!

ANDREY: You never think, and that's the truth!

IGOR: Oh well... (*Exits quickly to the passage.*)

IRENA: The poor man. Masha was right to help him.

OLGA: At least we're rid of him. That's one good thing.

(*Silence. IRENA looks through the window. She coughs behind her hand. ANDREY covers his eyes with his hand.*)

ANDREY: My violin... I feel so sorry for my poor violin... when I gave it to the man...when he took it with his big, red hands...it was like abandoning a little animal.

OLGA: Never mind. It's only a violin. A violin can't feel.

ANDREY: And when I looked back...it looked so small and lost. (*Bursts into tears.*)

(*MASHA goes to ANDREY and strokes his hair.*)

OLGA: (*Getting up.*) Come on. We must be quick. We can't be late. And we can't walk very fast because Irena will never keep up.

IRENA: There's nothing wrong with me.

NATASHA: (*Enters from the passage. She is overdressed and wearing a large hat with a veil. She is carrying a big suitcase and a hatbox.*) I hope you're finished. But as I know you...

OLGA: Are you completley stupid? How can you carry all that?

ANDREY: And don't think I'm going to carry it!

NATASHA: That's just what I'd expect of you.

IRENA: The man at the station told Andrey that there wasn't much space on the train. We can only take a small bundle each.

NATASHA: So! Do you want me to arrive in Moscow without any clothes?

MASHA: You can buy clothes there.

NATASHA: I suppose you think my clothes aren't good enough for your important friends? I'm not budging without my things! That you must know!

ANDREY: But there isn't space for all this stuff! They'll just throw it off the train!

NATASHA: That'll be the day!

ANDREY: And just look at you. Ridiculously toffed-up! Do you imagine you're going to the theatre?

OLGA: Well...if you don't mind me saying...you'll draw far too much attention to us. We're all trying to look like ordinary people.

NATASHA: 'Ordinary people'. Excuse me. What else do you think you are? You've always been so high-and-mighty. Thinking you were better than everyone else. And I've never been good enough for you. When I came here the first day you said 'Natasha, what a funny green belt you're wearing. I really don't think you should wear a belt like that.'

OLGA: I can't remember that at all.

NATASHA: And I've never forgotten it! Never! Like this! (*Illustrates.*) With your long nose in the air. (*Illustrates. Suddenly sees the sheets on the floor.*) And just look at that! No one has any respect for me! (*Storms out into the passage without her suitcase or her hatbox.*)
(*Short silence.*)

OLGA: Andrey, you must go and talk to her.

ANDREY: Why must I go?

OLGA: Because she's your wife. You married her, you idiot. Take all these things and go and talk to her. Try and calm her down. We don't have any time to waste.

MASHA: Yes, Olga's right. It's getting very late.

ANDREY: (*Unwilling.*) But you can see how angry she is...

IRENA: Come Andrusha, I'll go with you. (*Picking up the hatbox.*) Come now, you must take the suitcase.

ANDREY: (*Picking up the suitcase.*) This is going to break my back. It's as heavy as lead.

(*IRENA and ANDREY exit to the passage.*)

ANDREY: (*Off.*) What can she have in this thing...

(*Silence. OLGA rubs her eyes. MASHA goes to the window and looks out.*

The sound of shots being fired some distance away.)

OLGA: (*Almost as if she is speaking to herself.*) I dozed off for an hour or so... I was just lying on top of the bed... and of course I started feeling chilly. When I'm chilly, I always have the same dream. I dream about many people in a room. A big, empty room filled with powdery grey light. I'm in the middle of the room and all the people are looking at me. Such...strange people. And always people I've never seen before. (*Sighing.*) Oh, well...

MASHA: (*Turns and looks at OLGA.*) Olya...

(*OLGA closes her eyes.*)

Olya...

OLGA: (*She opens her eyes again. Smoothes down her dress.*) Our life...our old life is gone, isn't it? (*Looks at MASHA.*)

(*MASHA turns back to the window and looks out.*)

(*Looks down at her hands.*) Everything gone...

MASHA: Olya. (*She looks at OLGA.*) I'm so sorry.

OLGA: (*Tearfully.*) Oh, Masha, it's not you. It's much bigger than you or I. It's the end of the world, that's all. (*Softly.*) The end of the world.

(*OLGA and MASHA look at each other.*)

IRENA: (*Off.*) Masha! (*Enters quickly from the passage breathlessly.*) Alexander is sitting under the window on the terrace. Please call him to come up. Say you want to talk to him. Please Mashenka. You can call him through the window.

MASHA: Yes, I'll call him.

(*OLGA exits quickly to the bedroom and closes the door softly behind her.*)

(*Moves to the window and leans out.*) Oh... I'd almost
forgotten about the sweet air. (*Inhales deeply.*)

IRENA: Come on now, Mashenka.

MASHA: Yes...yes... (*Leans out, calling.*) Vershinin!
Vershinin! Please come up here! I would really like to
talk to you! (*Turning to IRENA.*) He's coming.

IRENA: (*Quickly and nervously.*) Tell him he must come to
Moscow soon. Tell him...that we can't bear to be without
him...and that I'll miss him much too much. Will you
tell him that?

MASHA: Yes. But you must go now. I'll talk to him alone.

IRENA: Thank you Mashenka (*Kisses MASHA on her cheek
and exits quickly to the bedroom, closing the door behind her.*)

MASHA: (*Moves about slowly. Hums and then starts singing.*)
'A green oak grows near the sea,
and around the trunk there is a golden chain...
and around the trunk there is a golden chain...'
I think I must be going mad. (*Little laugh.*)
'A green oak...near the sea...' Where did that come
from?

(*VERSHININ enters from the passage. He seems a little
dazed. He is dressed in the uniform of a white army general.
He is wearing two medals on his chest.*)

Vershinin...my dear Vershinin...that's how a General
should look. Come and sit here with me. Please, come
and sit.

(*VERSHININ goes and sits next to MASHA on the sofa.*)

I want to talk to you about Irena. You know she's not
been very well and I'm so worried about her. How is she
ever going to survive in Moscow? She so badly wants to
see our old house in Staraya Basmanyana Street. Have
I told you what our house has become?

(*VERSHININ nods.*)

A brothel. And you can hear the tinny piano through
the closed windows. Anyway... (*Putting her hand on
VERSHININ's arm.*) The only thing that can help her is
the belief that she'll see you in Moscow. You know how
she feels about you. My dear Vershinin...

VERSHININ: Come now, Masha. What do you want of me? I know you.

MASHA: (*Sad little laugh.*) Yes, you do. Strange, but you know me almost better than anyone else. I want to ask you to tell a little lie. To give Irena hope.

VERSHININ: (*Nodding.*) Of course.

MASHA: As long as she expects you she'll have something to live for. (*Little laugh.*) We all need that, don't we? (*Getting up.*) I'll go and call her.
(*Short silence. She looks down at her hands.*)
Thank you, my dear. (*Goes to the door and knocks.*) Irena! Irena!
(*IRENA opens the door. MASHA whispers something to her and then goes into the bedroom and closes the door behind her.*)

IRENA: (*Moves slowly into the room and then waits uncertainly. After a short silence.*) I have to go and dress Nana Anfisa. The people from the hospital will be fetching her soon.
(*A short silence and then IRENA moves quickly to the kitchen.*)

VERSHININ: Irena!

IRENA: (*Stops and looks at VERSHININ.*) Yes, Alexander?

VERSHININ: (*Without looking at her.*) I wanted to say... well, I hope there's enough space for me in Moscow... because I intend to get there one of these days.

IRENA: (*Moving to him.*) Oh, Alexander, I'm so glad. (*Sitting next to him on the sofa.*) So very glad.
(*Short silence.*)
(*Looking away.*) I hope it's very soon...we'll miss you very much.

VERSHININ: I'll miss all of you too.

IRENA: (*Turns to VERSHININ. Quick and breathless.*) You know me Alexander... I'm very shy and timid...and I know I'm not young any more... I know I've lost my looks...and an attractive man like you can have anyone he wants... (*Puts her hands in front of her face. Talking with her hands in front of her face.*) Alexander...you know what I'm trying to say...
(*A heavy silence. VERSHININ looks uncomfortable.*)

VERSHININ: My dear, good Irena...

(*IRENA drops her hands and looks at him.*)
(*Takes IRENA's face between his hands. He kisses her on her forehead. While he continues to talk, he holds her face in his hands. Tenderly.*) I think it's very late. Maybe you should get ready...
(*IRENA pulls her head away and gets up quickly. For a moment she stands motionless and closes her eyes very tightly. Then she opens her eyes and exits to the kitchen.*
Silence. VERSHININ takes a hip-flask out of his pocket and drinks deeply.)
(*Softly.*) Life...life... (*Puts the flask back.*)

SOFJA: (*Enters from the passage. Sees VERSHININ.*) I've been walking through all the old rooms. Looking at everything... I don't want to forget anything... I was born here and I've never lived anywhere else. Will we ever come back here, uncle Alexander? Tell me. (*Sits next to him.*)

VERSHININ: Maybe. I don't know. But even if you come back...nothing will ever be the same. Time changes everything.

SOFJA: How can I bear it, uncle Alexander? (*Tearfully.*) I feel as if my heart is breaking... (*Puts her head against his shoulder.*)

VERSHININ: (*Stroking her hair.*) Poor little Sofoshka. Life isn't easy. (*Putting his arm around her.*) There's so much that you don't know yet. You have your whole life in front of you...and my life is over. (*Little laugh.*) Poor uncle Alexander.
(*Short silence.*)
Oh well... (*Gets up with difficulty.*) There's something I would like to give to you. Maybe you can learn something from my miserable life. (*Goes to the table.*)

IRENA: (*Getting up.*) What is it, uncle Alexander? (*Goes to the table.*)

VERSHININ: (*Picking up his diary.*) It's the story of my life. If you read it, you'll see how many misfortunes one can actually survive. (*Little laugh.*) It's surprising really. There you are. It's yours. (*Gives the book to her.*)

SOFJA: Thank you, uncle Alexander. (*Taking the book and presses it against her chest.*) I'll always treasure it.

VERSHININ: (*Sitting at the table.*) Strange...it's often the small, unimportant things that one remembers best...
(*SOFJA also sits at the table. She puts the book on the table in front of her.*)
For instance...there's one memory that's always stayed with me...and it's become even clearer with time... One night, in Poland, my men and I found refuge in a small, deserted house...there was only a woman in the house and a sleeping child. A single lamp was burning and...

ANDREY: (*Off.*) Sofja! (*Enters. Breathless.*) Your mother's looking for you. She said you must come and put on your hat and get your things together.

SOFJA: Yes. (*Jumping up.*) I suppose it's time to go...
(*ANDREY falls into a chair.*)
Are you coming to see us off uncle Alexander?

VERSHININ: (*Getting up.*) I don't think so. I think I'll stay here.
(*IRENA and ANFISA enter from the kitchen. IRENA is holding ANFISA's arm. ANFISA is dressed in a clean nightdress and a nightcap.*)

ANFISA: (*Confused. Looking at IRENA.*) Is it very late?

IRENA: Yes, it is. (*While the others continue to talk she leads ANFISA to the child's bed and helps her onto the bed.*)

SOFJA: Please stand at the window uncle Alexander. We're taking the short-cut through the garden and we can turn around and wave at you.

VERSHININ: Yes, I'll stand at the window.

SOFJA: (*Putting her hands on VERSHININ's shoulders.*)
And you must watch until you can't see us any more. (*Kisses him on the cheek. Goes to ANFISA.*) Bye-bye dearest Nana. (*Kisses her on her cheek and exits quickly to the passage.*)
(*VERSHININ sees the exercise book on the table. He picks it up and looks at the door as if he wants to call SOFJA back. Then, slowly, he puts it down again.*)

IRENA: There we are, Nana. Let me put the pillow behind your back.

OLGA: (*Opening the bedroom door.*) Irena, please come and make sure that you haven't forgotten anything important.

(*IRENA goes to the bedroom.*)

ANDREY: (*Takes out his pocket-watch and looks at it.*) It's
stopped again. If it hadn't been Pappa's, I would have
sold the bloody thing.
(*VERSHININ looks out of the window.*)
(*Getting up.*) Well my friend, I suppose it's time to go.
(*Going to VERSHININ.*) My dear fellow... (*Embraces him
and bangs him on the back with both hands.*) Maybe it's not
that bad... (*Laughs.*) Maybe I'll become a professor after
all. (*Laughs.*) Well... (*Suddenly moved. Walking away.*)
(*OLGA and IRENA enter with bundles. OLGA is carrying
a parasol.*)

IRENA: (*To OLGA.*) We can pretend that we're only going
for a picnic.

OLGA: (*Distracted.*) Yes...yes...that's a good idea.

IRENA: Then we'll be happy until we get to the station.

ANDREY: (*Bending over.*) Goodbye Nana! (*Louder.*) Goodbye
Nana!

ANFISA: (*Looking up slowly.*) And who are you?
(*ANDREY looks rather lost. He remains motionless for a
moment and then wanders off to the passage.*)

OLGA: (*Putting out her hand.*) All the best, Alexander
Ignatevich.

VERSHININ: (*Shaking her hand.*) And god bless you, Olga
Sergeyevna.

OLGA: I only hope I can get to the station. I have to walk
so far and I'm as blind as a bat. (*Looking at IRENA.*)
Irena, your hat! Your hat!
(*IRENA puts down her bundle and exits to the bedroom.*)
I can only see things very close to me...anything else
seems to fade away. Oh well, maybe I'll be able to get
some glasses in Moscow. (*Moves to ANFISA. Touches her
shoulder.*) Thank you for everything, dear Nana.
(*IRENA enters with her hat in her hand.*)

IRENA: (*Formal. Without looking at him.*) Goodbye
Alexander.

VERSHININ: Goodbye Irena Sergeyevna.

IRENA: (*To ANFISA.*) Dear Nana Anfisa, I must say goodbye
now. Please look at me. Look at me...

ANIFSA: (*Looks at her. After a short silence.*) And who are you? I don't know you.

IRENA: Please know me Nana. Please know me. (*Weeping.*) Just this once...

OLGA: Come, we're just wasting time. I hope I'm not talking out of turn, Vershinin, but I really think you must take off that uniform. If you're seen like that, it won't do you any good.

(*IRENA is holding ANFISA and crying bitterly.*)

(*Goes to IRENA and pulls her away.*) Come now, we have to go. Leave her. You have to. (*Takes IRENA's arm and leads her to the door. IRENA is still crying.*)

(*OLGA and IRENA exit to the passage.*)

(*Off.*) Masha! Please bring Irena's bundle! And be quick!

MASHA: (*Off. From the bedroom.*) I won't be long!

VERSHININ: (*Talking to himself.*) It was on a day just like this...a bright sunny day...that I came here for the first time...

(*Sound of shots and answering shots being fired.*)

ANDREY: (*Peering around the door.*) By the way, Vershinin old fellow... I'm sorry to trouble you...but someone's just sent a message to tell us that the people from the hospital can only fetch old Anfisa in a few days' time. There are too many wounded. I don't want the women to find out. You know what they're like. Oh well...maybe you can ask the Onegin's to keep an eye on her... I have to be going now... (*Disappears again.*)

(*VERSHININ looks dazed as if he has not heard a word. MASHA enters from the bedroom with a small suitcase and a bundle. She is wearing a hat with a veil. She turns, looks into the mirror and then she goes towards VERSHININ.*)

MASHA: Dear Vershinin...

(*VERSHININ turns his head and looks at her.*)

Let's not say goodbye. (*Puts down the bundle, presses her two fingers against her mouth and then touches VERSHININ's forehead. She picks up the bundle and exits to the passage.*)

(*Silence. VERSHININ gets up slowly. Suddenly he looks resolute. He goes to the toy cupboard and starts looking for something. He finds the jack-in-a-box and opens it. The jack-in-the-box jumps out. He shakes the box and bullets roll out onto the table. He hears someone on the stairs. He puts the box back in the cupboard and the bullets in his pocket.)*

SOFJA: (*Enters breathlessly.*) Just imagine what I forgot!
(VERSHININ smiles and picks up the exercise book to give to SOFJA. SOFJA exits into the bedroom.)
(Off.) Aunt Olga's canary!
(VERSHININ slowly puts the book down again.)
(Enters with a bird cage covered with a shawl.) I told her I'd bring it down, but I quite forgot! Remember to wave, uncle Alexander. (*Exits quickly. Off.*) I'm coming!
(VERSHININ remains motionless for a moment, then he goes towards the child's bed and starts feeling for something under the mattress.)
(Calling from the garden.) Goodbye uncle Alexander! Goodbye!

ANDREY: (*Calling from the garden.*) Goodbye old fellow!
(VERSHININ finds the gun. He goes to the table and sits down.)

CHORUS OF VOICES: (*Further off.*) Goodbye! Goodbye!
(VERSHININ smoothes down his uniform. He looks down at his medals and then he shines one of his medals with his sleeve. He starts loading the gun.)

VERSHININ: When they find me, I want them to say 'He was a brave soldier, even if he was our enemy.' (*After a while he stops loading the gun and puts it down. He looks at the gun. After a time he picks it up again but then puts it down. Wry little laugh. Gets up very slowly.*) But I'm just a coward…a gutless fool… (*His face contorts. He pulls off his medals and throws them onto the table. He looks slightly dazed, then he moves slowly to the window and looks out.*) There they are, old Anfisa. Getting smaller and smaller and soon they'll disappear completely. (*Slight silence. Softly.*) Those bastards won't find me here, trapped like a rat. I won't skulk and hide, that I won't do. No, old Anfisa, you know me better than that. (*He turns slowly.*) The last time I left, it was a cold autumn day…and the trees were bare…

I was leaving behind the woman I loved...and yet I felt excited. Girls were waving their handkerchiefs and the military band was playing... (*Seems to listen.*) I can almost hear it... (*Hums.*) Da da da da-da-da-da-da da... Da da da da-da-da-da-da da... (*Trails off.*) This time... everything's different. No...no...not everything. I'm Alexander Ignatevich Vershinin. (*Looks at the door.*) And I'm...marching into battle again. (*Starts moving towards the door. Feels in his breast pocket and takes out a half jack of Vodka. He holds it up to the light and sees that it is half full. Makes a sound expressing satisfaction. Opens the bottle and drinks as he slowly exits.*)

(*After a few moments the sound of an explosion. ANFISA has a fright and opens her eyes wide.*)

ANFISA: (*Listening intently.*) And why is it so quiet?

(*Listens.*) You're hiding from me again. You don't want to come and bath, you naughty children. (*Calls.*) Come on out, children! Come on out! Or else I'll go and tell your Mamma! And then you'll really be in trouble!

(*ANFISA stares out in front of her.*

The sound of shots being fired in the distance. After a few seconds the sound of an explosion as the lights slowly fade to black.)

The End.

YELENA

in memory of my gifted mother and grandmother

'Uncle Vanya says I have mermaid's blood in my veins. "Let yourself go"... Well, perhaps that's what I ought to do... To fly away, free as a bird, away from all your sleepy faces and your talk, to forget you exist at all – every one of you!'

Yelena, Chekhov's *Uncle Vanya*

'You're a sly one... You charming bird of prey... A beautiful, furry animal... Here I am, devour me!'

Astrov to Yelena, Chekhov's *Uncle Vanya*

Characters

MIKHAIL ASTROV
forty-five, a country doctor

SONYA ALEXANDREVNA
thirty, his wife, daughter of the late
Professor Serebryakov

YELENA ANDREYEVNA
thirty-five, Sonya's Stepmother and widow of
Professor Serebrayakov

IVAN PETROVICH
fifty-two, (Uncle Vanya), Sonya's maternal uncle

ILYA TELEGIN
sixty-eight, Sonya's Godfather, an elderly impoverished
landowner who lives in a cottage on the estate

The Action takes place eight years after the conclusion of
Anton Chekhov's *Uncle Vanya*, during the spring, the
summer and the autumn of 1905

Yelena was first performed at the The State Theatre in Pretoria on 10 August 1998 and was produced by The State Theatre and Dalro, with the following cast:

ASTROV,   Graham Hopkins

SONYA,   Charlotte Butler

YELENA,   Jana Cilliers

VANYA,   Frantz Dobrowsky

TELEGIN,   Norman Coombes

Director,   Marthinus Basson

Setting

The drawing room in a seedy country house once owned by the late professor Serebryakov, now owned by Sonya and her husband, Dr Astrov. The room is claustrophobic and gloomy. The heavy furniture seems to loom out of the shadows. There is a narrow window seat underneath the windows. All the scenes take place at night and for this reason it is always dark outside. Because of the blackness outside, the large windows in the back wall dimly reflect the action taking place in the room. The study door is right centre, the hall door is left back and the dining room door is left front. In the centre right is a sagging sofa with sorry-looking velvet and brocade pillows in each corner. Two mismatched armchairs are front left and right of the sofa. Next to the sofa, on the left, there is a small side-table. Left in the middle there is a fair-sized round table. The table is covered by a fringed cloth. There are four heavily-carved chairs at the table. Suspended above the table is an oil lamp with an ochre shade. Left, against the wall, there is a heavy sideboard.

It is vital that the set is shadowy and that there is strong contrast between light and shadow. The set is mainly illuminated by a single source of light (the lamp above the table). It illuminates the part of the room and the characters adjacent to it. If the characters move away, only one side of their face will be in the light or they will be seen only dimly. Other sources of light are the bright moon in Act Two, which shines through the windows at the back and casts long shadows across the stage and the garish flickering torches seen through the window toward the end of the play. Wavering, weak, ghostly light also spills through the doorways leading into the drawing room.

Sound effects

These are integral to the orchestration of the play and should be used precisely as directed. The sound effects must sound entirely life-like.

Music

No other music must be heard during or before the play, except Telegin's playing and the 'Presto' movement from Scriabin's Piano Sonata no.2 in G sharp minor. This music is not optional and forms an integral part of the play.

ACT ONE

When the lights go up only the lamp above the table is lit. It flickers from time to time until the window is closed. Fairly dim candle light spills onto the stage from the open door leading to VANYA's study as well as from the open hall door. There is a sewing basket on the couch. A cold, softly whistling wind can be heard. It is heard throughout the act. SONYA is sitting at the table. She is busy darning a sock. The sewing basket is on the table in front of her. YELENA is reclining on the sofa. She is wearing a dark green dress with a train. Her abundant hair looks somewhat dishevelled.

Short silence.

SONYA: Is your headache any better?

YELENA: (*Opening her eyes.*) Yes... Yes. You were right.
    That's what I needed. To lie down for a while. (*Sits up
    slowly.*) In fact, it's almost gone.
    (*Short silence.*)

SONYA: Oh... I'm so sleepy... I should really go to bed.
    But somehow... I always feel restless and worried until
    Astrov gets home.

YELENA: And how is he?

SONYA: Tired. Very tired. There's a Cholera epidemic in
    town.
    (*YELENA sighs and closes her eyes. SONYA watches her as
    she continues to sew.*)

YELENA: (*Suddenly opening her eyes.*) Why do you look at
    me like that?

SONYA: I'm not looking at you.

YELENA: (*Sitting up.*) It's no use pretending. I saw the look
    in your eyes.

SONYA: That's not true!

YELENA: (*Getting up and moving about restlessly as if talking
    to herself.*) Imagine that... Sonya pitying *me*...So this is
    what its come to? It is simply too...grotesque.

SONYA: (*Tearful.*) I watched you...because I'm so glad to
    see you!

YELENA: I really can't blame you, dear Sonya. I really can't. After all...I used to be quite lovely. Well...at least I haven't lost my figure. I'm...quite as trim as ever.
(*VANYA enters from the study. He is wearing a dressing gown and old slippers.*)

VANYA: I can't sleep! I've tried, but I can't. When I close my eyes, I see sparks of light and my ears start humming. And I still can't find that book I was looking for. Things just disappear. They do. And you never find them again. (*Puts his hand over his eyes.*)

SONYA: What's wrong, Uncle Vanya?

VANYA: Suddenly I feel so strange...

SONYA: Come now, let me get you back to bed.

VANYA: Oh, it's no use. I feel too restless.

YELENA: It must be the wind.

SONYA: When I was making tea I heard it howling in the chimney. (*Shudders.*) That's how it sounded...exactly like that...before father died. (*Sits down. Takes another sock out of the sewing basket and starts darning.*)

VANYA: I dropped off about half an hour ago, but something strange woke me up... I don't know what it was. A little wine or Vodka used to help me sleep. But now it only wakes me up.

SONYA: Maybe it was Yelena walking about upstairs. Her train was dragging across the floor. (*To YELENA.*) Dear Yelena, you've brought these impractical fashionable dresses to the country again.

YELENA: Hardly 'fashionable'. I've become one of those pitiful women who say 'I have the cleverest little seamstress. A real jewel. She can do wonders with last year's dresses'.
(*Short silence.*)

SONYA: (*Sighs. Continues to darn.*) I don't know why Astrov is so late. He said he would be back by ten. (*Angry. Throwing the sock back into the basket.*) That's the third time I've had to darn that sock. It's simply no use! How sick I am of this scrimping and saving. Sick and tired...

VANYA: Maybe he took Telegin home first. (*Strange laugh.*) Poor old Telegin. Bad things always seem to happen to the best people. (*Moves towards the dining room.*)

SONYA: Where are you going, Uncle?

VANYA: I thought... Just a small nightcap.

SONYA: But you said yourself...

VANYA: I really don't feel well tonight... My nerves are very bad...

SONYA: But you promised!

VANYA: I'm not a child. Don't treat me like a child! You should stop worrying about me and do something about your husband. This morning I saw him drinking before breakfast.
(*SONYA gives a shuddering sigh and turns her head away.*)
Oh well... I suppose it doesn't matter. The fellow must do as he likes.
(*Silence.*)
There now... Don't upset yourself. I won't touch a drop, I promise.

SONYA: (*Lifting her head and looking at him.*) It's not that... It's... I don't know... These last weeks have seemed so strange... I don't know how to explain...

VANYA: Yes... They have seemed rather peculiar.

SONYA: That sudden, unnatural heat... The Cholera epidemic... Telegin's mad wife arriving out of the blue. After all those years...

VANYA: (*Laughs.*) Dreadful old hag. Poor Telegin.

SONYA: And then... Yelena. (*Smiles at YELENA.*) Coming back to us so unexpectedly.

YELENA: I know. To give you almost no warning. It was really inexcusable of me.

SONYA: Now, you mustn't say that. We're so very glad to have you. Isn't that true Uncle?

VANYA: (*To YELENA.*) I should never have answered your letter.

SONYA: But Uncle! How can you say that!

VANYA: Well, that's as much as she deserves. (*Laughs.*)

SONYA: He's only teasing you. You remember what he's like.

VANYA: (*Moves about restlessly.*) I assure you... I'm quite serious. (*Laughs.*) After your poor father died, I kept sending your stepmother (*Indicates YELENA.*) an allowance as you know.

YELENA: And I've always been very grateful...

VANYA: And each time, I also wrote her a letter. Every month...for two years. But I never heard from her. Not even once.

YELENA: I'm so sorry. I kept meaning to write.

VANYA: Weeks...months...years. And still every day when the postman came, I trembled and my heart started beating wildly. My God, I was so pathetic. (*Shrugs.*)

SONYA: Oh, Uncle...

YELENA: It's just that I didn't know what to say.

VANYA: Often I dreamt about getting a letter. I would be so happy. So deliriously happy. But I could never make out the words in my dream. (*Laughs.*)

SONYA: I never thought... I never imagined... Now I understand... So that's why you started drinking after they left, uncle. And you didn't seem to care about anything.

VANYA: I couldn't even talk to anybody. I was too ashamed. She was your stepmother after all. And I'm an old fool.

SONYA: (*Tearfully.*) Oh, poor uncle. If only I'd known. And to think I was always scolding you for being lazy and thoughtless.

YELENA: You're making me feel so dreadful...

VANYA: (*Laughs.*) So you see... That's why I should have torn up her letter when it came. Torn it up into a thousand pieces.

YELENA: And why didn't you?

VANYA: Well, you told me about your difficult circumstances. About how ill you'd been. And then, I thought, what harm can it do? I'm quite over it now. Quite over it now. It's been eight years since I've seen you, after all.

SONYA: So long...

YELENA: And can you forgive me, Ivan Petrovich? For being so selfish. So thoughtless.

VANYA: Oh Yelena Andreyevna. (*Laughs.*) I forgave you long ago.

(*The wind howls.*)

Just listen to that. It's enough to drive you insane! What a vile climate we have! Vile! I've often said it and I'll say it again. It's only fit for wild beasts.

SONYA: Well at least summer's not far off.

VANYA: Vile!

(*The wind drops again.*)

SONYA: Come and sit down Uncle. You're working yourself up into a dreadful state.

(*Silence. VANYA sits down heavily.*)

YELENA: If only you knew how unhappy I've been. How ill and alone. Then maybe you would be able to understand.

VANYA: Come now Yelena Andreyevna. I've told you it's forgotten. All in the past.

SONYA: The only important thing is for you to get better.

VANYA: Quite right. And you will. We have as much fresh air as you need.

YELENA: You're so kind to me.

VANYA: Nonsense... Nonsense.

(*Silence.*

(*YELENA leans back and closes her eyes. SONYA darns. VANYA suddenly goes to the dresser and opens the drawers rather violently. He rummages through them.*)

This is the last place I haven't looked. But it's not here. Simply vanished, as I said.

SONYA: Nonsense Uncle. We'll find the book tomorrow.

(*Yawns.*) I'm so sleepy, I can hardly see out of my eyes.

(*VANYA shuts the drawers loudly.*)

YELENA: (*Sitting up.*) Oh, before I forget... Could you get me another candle to take upstairs, Sonya dear? I know it's childish, but I'm afraid of the dark. And the one in my room has burnt down rather low.

SONYA: Of course. Just remind me.

YELENA: (*Laughs.*) And just look at my hair. I think I've dropped my hairpins all over the house. You see... I've been walking about upstairs... Looking at the old rooms.

VANYA: Twenty-six rooms. Imagine that. We've never known what to do with them. (*Laughs.*) It's simply ridiculous.

SONYA: I feel a draft. Someone left the window a little open. Won't you close it Uncle. It's making the lamp flicker.

VANYA: (*Going to close the window.*) Most of the rooms are damp. They smell like caves. (*Closing the window.*) The roof leaks in a thousand places and there are death watch beetles in the walls.

YELENA: (*Looking around.*) Everything looks familiar and yet so...strange...

VANYA: I'm afraid you weren't happy here.

YELENA: Well now, that's not exactly true...

VANYA: You thought we were a bunch of ignorant country bumpkins. Come now. Admit it.

SONYA: Uncle! Stop it! He's only teasing you.

YELENA: (*Moving about.*) I was unhappy. That's true. But it had nothing to do with you. You were all so kind to me. No, no... It's just that I'm an unhappy woman. (*Laughs.*) An unhappy woman of no importance. (*Peering into the dining room.*) Is the old piano still in there?

SONYA: Yes. But no one ever touches it.

YELENA: Your father never wanted me to play. Do you remember?

SONYA: Yes. You always sent me to ask him if you could. But he was always feeling too unwell.

YELENA: How he detested my playing.

VANYA: You can play something for us now. While we're waiting for the doctor.

YELENA: I don't know. I haven't played for so long...

SONYA: Please do.

VANYA: Only music can bring the sublime and mysterious into our ordinary lives.

SONYA: Please play.

YELENA: If only I could play as I used to. (*Looks at her hands.*) Once, when I was studying at the conservatory at St Petersburg, I was asked to give a short recital. At first I was very nervous. But then...when I started to play... I seemed to...lose myself. To... (*Short laugh.*) It's really difficult to explain...

SONYA: Please play. There is a candle in the dining-room. If you need more light... I'll come and light the candles in the candelabra.

YELENA: Very well. (*She goes into the dining room.*)

VANYA: (*Softly to SONYA.*) I thought it was all over. I really did. But I might as well admit it...

(*YELENA can be heard playing a scale, the piano is out of tune.*)

When I saw her at the station this morning... So thin and pale... And I took her hands in mine. Like two frozen birds. (*He puts his hand over his eye.*) I felt as if I'd been poisoned again.

SONYA: Oh, Uncle...

VANYA: Yes...yes. I can feel the poison coursing through my veins.

(*The sound of the piano lid being closed.*)

I don't think she's going to play after all.

YELENA: (*Enters with the candle.*) I'm afraid it's out of tune. (*Sound of a horse and cart approaching.*)

And the keys are so dusty. (*Wipes her hand on her dress.*)

SONYA: Thank goodness. There they are (*To YELENA.*) I'm glad you're still up. Astrov has been looking forward to seeing you.

YELENA: Has he changed much?

SONYA: Oh well...he's older of course. As we all are.

YELENA: I really think I would rather see him tomorrow. I didn't sleep last night. Who can sleep in a train? And my hair... I really look a fright.

SONYA: He's extremely exhausted. He won't even notice. (*ASTROV's voice can be heard in the hall.*)

Anyway...it's too late.

(*ASTROV appears in the door. He is wearing a rather dusty corduroy suit.*)

ASTROV: Yelena Andreyevna... I thought you'd be asleep when I got back.

VANYA: Well, she's not. So there you are.

(*ASTROV goes to YELENA and kisses her hand.*)

ASTROV: I'm sorry my lips are so cold. But I'm half-frozen.

YELENA: You've trimmed your moustache, doctor. It was much longer. It used to make you look so dismal.

ASTROV: (*Laughs.*) Well, I'm glad I look less dismal.

YELENA: (*Laughs.*) But you still smell of carbolic soap.

ASTROV: I suppose I do.

(*TELEGIN appears in the door. He is wearing a shabby suit and is carrying a small parcel.*)

TELEGIN: Telegin. Illya Illyich. I don't suppose you remember me Yelena Andreyevna?

(*ASTROV goes to the dining room.*)

YELENA: My dear Telegin. Of course I do.

TELEGIN: Everything will be better now, won't it Ivan Petrovich? Yelena Andrayevna is back again!

VANYA: It certainly will. It certainly will my friend.

(*ASTROV emerges from the dining room with two glasses of vodka.*)

ASTROV: (*Giving the glass to TELEGIN.*) Drink this.

TELEGIN: On doctors orders?

ASTROV: Absolutely. (*Knocks back his vodka.*)

(*TELEGIN puts his parcel down and drinks his vodka.*)

VANYA: That reminds me doctor. I also need you to give me something. I can't sleep.

ASTROV: Laudanum. That should do it.

(*TELEGIN sits down on the couch.*)

SONYA: (*Irritable.*) Please don't sit down, Godfather dear.

(*TELEGIN looks confused and gets up again.*)

You're simply covered in dust. You should dust yourself off in the hall. I've told you that often enough.

TELEGIN: (*Looks guilty.*) I'm sorry... Very sorry. (*Exits through the hall door.*)

VANYA: (*Harsh whisper.*) Must you always be so irritable with the poor man? He feels like a hanger-on as it is. And the way you spoke to him at dinner last night.

SONYA: (*Harsh whisper. Tearful.*) It's easy for you to say uncle. You don't have to rub the stains out of the tablecloth... You don't have to sweep and dust, sweep and dust...

VANYA: Ssh.

(*TELEGIN appears in the door.*)

Come and sit down old friend. Don't worry about this nonsense.

TELEGIN: (*Hovering in the door.*) Never mind... Never mind... I can't stay for very long...

(*Short silence.*)

We've been so lonely here Yelena Andreyevna. The house has been so empty. Old Nanny Marina going blind and then Maria Vasiliyevna dying so suddenly. I found her, you know. (*Points.*) Sitting in that chair. Her eyes were wide open.

SONYA: Poor granny. And on the floor all around her were those pamphlets she used to read. About Women's emancipation.

YELENA: (*To VANYA.*) I'm so sorry about your mother. I never knew. Nobody wrote and told me.

VANYA: Well, you never answered any of my letters as you know. So I stopped writing.

ASTROV: Never mind. She didn't answer my letters either.

SONYA: You wrote to her?

YELENA: (*Quickly.*) Some very kind and sympathetic letters. After your father's death. (*To ASTROV,*) I'm very sorry. I kept meaning to write. I wrote so many letters in my head...

TELEGIN: Things have been getting very difficult around here Yelena Andreyevna. I can tell you that. Everyone snapping at each other like a pack of curs.

ASTROV: We were expecting you two days ago.

YELENA: I'm afraid I had to ask Ivan Petrovich to telegraph me some money. You see... I found that I didn't have enough money to buy a ticket. I've had so many medical expenses...

VANYA: (*Interrupting her.*) Oh, let's not talk about that.

(*ASTROV out to the dining-room.*)

TELEGIN: And the fares have gone up so dreadfully. It really is quite scandalous.

(*SONYA follows ASTROV to the dining-room.*)

VANYA: I don't know if we've told you Yelena Andreyevna, but Telegin's wife has returned to him after forty six years.

ASTROV: (*Raised voice from the dining-room.*) Can't you ever leave me alone!

(*Short silence.*)

YELENA: Oh, I'm very glad for you.

SONYA: (*Tearful voice from the dining-room.*) But you know that if you start you can't stop!

TELEGIN: Oh well, I think I'd better get back to her. The poor soul will be waiting for me. She cries when I leave her alone. Whimpers like a little puppy.

(*ASTROV enters with a glass of vodka.*)

VANYA: Telegin is just going.

TELEGIN: Well yes... I'll see you all tomorrow. Goodbye then.

YELENA: Goodbye.

VANYA: Goodbye old friend.

ASTROV: Goodbye. Regards to the wife.

(*A short silence.*)

Can you imagine? His wife suddenly reappears after forty six years. A dreadful old hag. (*Laughs.*) Completely gagga. (*Drinks.*)

VANYA: And she doesn't even know him. She calls him Sergei.

YELENA: Sergei?

ASTROV: The name of her former lover. The man she left him for.

VANYA: Imagine that!

(*SONYA enters from the dining-room. She looks tearful.*)

ASTROV: (*Imitating the wife.*) 'Sergei, Sergei, is that you?' (*Imitating TELEGIN.*) 'Yes my dear. Of course it is.' You should see her simpering and smiling. Showing her toothless gums. (*Drinks.*)

VANYA: Poor old Waffles.

ASTROV: The last time I was there, she sat on his lap and whispered endearments in his ear. (*Laughs.*) It really was grotesque.

VANYA: And he never complains.

SONYA: (*Still tearful.*) He's kind to her because he loves her!

ASTROV: (*Viciously.*) That's not love! It's pathetic! (*Puts down his glass.*)

(*Silence.*)

VANYA: Well Doctor, come and give me something to help me sleep. You said you would. (*Moves towards the study.*)

ASTROV: Yes. (*Picks up his bag and follows VANYA. He turns back at the door.*) I believe you'll be staying with us for some time, Yelena Andreyevna.

YELENA: If you can put up with me.

(*VANYA laughs.*)

ASTROV: Well, I'm afraid you won't find our company very inspiring. In fact, we've become the dreariest people on earth. (*Laughs, follows VANYA into the study.*)

(*Short silence.*)

SONYA: I can't imagine what you must think of us. You must understand... Things have been very difficult.

YELENA: Yes... But then... Things haven't been easy for me either. That's why I've lost my looks. No, don't say anything. I know I have. My youth is gone. Oh, let's not talk about it. I'm just an unfortunate woman. (*Little laugh.*) Do you remember when you told me about the doctor? That you loved him? It was in this very room and I said I would talk to him.

SONYA: I remember. And then he said he didn't want me and you told him not to come here any more.

YELENA: But you see... Everything has turned out well in the end.

(*SONYA turns her head away. Short silence.*)

Why is it so quiet? I don't remember the nights being as quiet as this?

SONYA: Oh, I know... It's because the watchman isn't tapping. He's very old now and he often falls asleep.

YELENA: (*Laughs.*) And now there's no-one to keep the evil spirits and the robbers away.

(*Short silence.*)

SONYA: I'm so happy that you're here.

YELENA: It seems such a long time ago... I'm quite a different person now, you know.

ASTROV: (*Appears in the study door. Coldly to SONYA.*) Could you get your uncle some water?

SONYA: (*Coldly.*) Very well. (*Gets up and goes to the dining-room.*)

ASTROV: (*To YELENA.*) I know I'm looking very unkempt. But I've been fighting a Cholera epidemic for eight weeks. And this evening I treated a poor woman who tried to poison herself for love. No-one knew what she'd taken, but I realised it was iodine. 'Illich, give me your hand' she kept moaning.

YELENA: And how did you know what it was?

ASTROV: The room had that peculiar smell. Like green walnuts.

(*SONYA quickly in and gives him the glass without looking at him.*)

Thank you. (*He goes back into the study.*)

(*Short silence.*)

SONYA: It's been so hard, you can hardly imagine. After you left, uncle started neglecting his duties. I had to do everything. All those accounts. Night after night I always seemed to have a headache... Then it rained for two years during autumn and all the hay rotted. And a year after that, I became very ill.

YELENA: Yes... I hope you don't mind, but this morning, on the way here, your uncle told me about your loss.

SONYA: A little boy. He was stillborn. Perfect as a doll. Astrov and I never talk about it. Once, about a year ago, he said that this was no world to bring a child into. That it was probably all for the best. (*Weeps.*)

YELENA: Come now... I'm sure he didn't mean it.

SONYA: He did. You should have heard him. (*Weeps.*)

YELENA: Please don't tell me these things. It's really none of my business my dear. I find it embarrassing. So distressing.

SONYA: But you're the only person I can talk to. I missed you so much when you left. But when you were here, I often wanted you to go away. Isn't that strange?

YELENA: How sulky you were. (*Laughs.*) Such black looks you used to give me. You thought I'd married your father for his money. Oh, my dear, if I'd wanted to marry for money, I could have done much better for myself, I can tell you. I can barely survive on the small allowance I get.

SONYA: I'm very sorry, but that's the best we can do.

YELENA: Of course... Of course. (*Coughs.*)

SONYA: If you only knew what it's cost us! When the farm was going to pieces, almost everything had to go to you! We hardly had anything to live on! But uncle Vanya would rather see us starve than inconvenience you!

YELENA: I should never have said anything! I don't know why I did. I'm always saying silly, unnecessary things. Please don't let's quarrel. It's late and I'm very tired.

SONYA: You're right.

YELENA: Friends?

SONYA: Friends. (*She kisses YELENA on the cheek.*)
(*Short silence.*)
I must go to bed. I have to be up early for the milking. Just look at my hands. All these calluses. How ugly they are. But without work, I don't think I would know what to do.
(*Sound of VANYA and ASTROV laughing in the study.*)
Are you coming up with me?

YELENA: I'll sit for a little while longer. I feel somehow too tired to move.

SONYA: (*Goes to the door. Turns at the door.*) Will you do something for me?

YELENA: Yes, of course.

SONYA: If Astrov comes out of the study will you please tell him that I need to speak to him. That I won't be able to sleep until I've spoken to him.

YELENA: I'll tell him.

SONYA: Goodnight then.

YELENA: Goodnight.
(*SONYA exits through the hall door. YELENA takes out her handkerchief and coughs.*)

ASTROV: (*Opens the door. He is carrying his bag. Calling back to VANYA.*) They said they couldn't pay me but they would give me a rat-trap!
(*VANYA laughs. ASTROV closes the study door.*)
(*Seeing her.*) Yelena Andreyevna.

YELENA: I was just going to bed. But I seem to be too tired to move.

ASTROV: Well, let me sit down for a minute. I haven't had a moment to myself all day. Do you mind if I smoke?

YELENA: Not at all.

(*Silence. ASTROV lights his cigarette.*)

Oh, I almost forgot. Sonya asked me to give you a message. She wants you to go upstairs at once. She wants to talk to you.

ASTROV: I'm sure she does.

(*Short silence.*)

YELENA: I never congratulated you.

ASTROV: And why should you do that?

YELENA: Well, you're a married man. I always thought Sonya would make a wonderful wife.

ASTROV: For a country doctor who smells of carbolic soap. (*Leaning forward.*) Was that why you never answered my letters. Was I not good enough for you?

YELENA: It's not that. I...just didn't know what to say.

(*Timid knock on the hall door. TELEGIN appears in the door.*)

TELEGIN: I'm sorry to disturb you, but I was halfway home when I remembered about my parcel. (*Picks up the parcel.*) That's why I went to town today. They cost me all my savings. I had them especially made. They're a set of teeth for my wife, you see. She can't eat properly. She has hardly any teeth left. Only a few stumps at the back. Well... I won't keep you then. Goodnight Doctor. Goodnight Yelena Andreyevna.

YELENA: Goodbye.

(*TELEGIN exits.*)

ASTROV: Imagine! (*He laughs.*)

(*Short silence.*)

I thought my feelings for you would vanish like that. (*Clicks his fingers.*) when you left. My God, I've dallied with enough women to know.

YELENA: (*Laughs.*) *La comedia e finito*! That's what you said when we left.

ASTROV: (*Laughs.*) That's what I always said. (*Short silence.*) But after you left I felt somehow...dazed...dazed. As if I was suffering from sunstroke.

YELENA: Please don't tell me these things.

ASTROV: That's when I realised what a dangerous woman you are. (*Short silence.*) Did you ever think of me? During all those years?

YELENA: Don't ask me these questions.

ASTROV: But did you? Did you ever spare me the slightest thought?

YELENA: Why are you hounding me like this? I'm so tired... I can hardly think. This makes me feel so awful... So guilty. Sonya is your wife now.

ASTROV: Once I found one of your hairpins in a crack in the floor. I kept it like a relic. Once I even put it into my mouth. On my tongue. I imagined that I could taste your hair.

YELENA: (*Getting up.*) This is unbearable. I should never have come back here.

ASTROV: And I suppose you never would have. But you need fresh country air. And a doctor who doesn't cost anything. (*Laughs.*) You must be careful. If you throw yourself on my mercy, I might take advantage of you.

YELENA: It's not true. I...need to be among friends. I've been so wretched. That's why I became ill. So wretched, because I realised that I'd wasted my youth, my best years, on Sonya's father the Professor. Wasted myself on that bloodless old man.

(*VANYA appears in the study door.*)

VANYA: Not any point in giving me laudanum if you're going to talk and keep me awake.

YELENA: I'm sorry. I was just going.

VANYA: (*Irritable.*) No, by all means. But as long as you go and talk somewhere else.

ASTROV: We were talking about old times. Catching up.

SONYA: (*Voice off.*) Astrov, won't you please come up to bed! I want to talk to you! I can't sleep, until I've talked to you!

ASTROV: I'm coming! Well, goodnight then Yelena Andreyevna. And you can rely on me. You'll have the best treatment I can give you.

YELENA: Thank you.

VANYA: (*Dismissing him.*) Goodnight. Goodnight. (*Calling to SONYA.*) By the way, I found that book I was looking for! (*ASTROV exits through the hall door.*) I found it under my bed, can you imagine! (*Short silence.*)

YELENA: Well, I must go up to bed.

VANYA: Oh please, Yelena Andreyevna. Give me just a few moments.

YELENA: I'm terribly tired. I haven't slept properly for a week. I feel a little demented.

VANYA: It's just that having you back here... Being under the same roof... I can hardly believe it. Even now. Looking at you.

YELENA: It's strange for me too. Coming back here.

VANYA: I've grown old, I know. I've become an old man.

YELENA: It's not true.

VANYA: But you haven't changed. You are still the most beautiful...most enchanting creature in the world. The most...adorable.

YELENA: But I thought you said all that was in the past.

VANYA: I only said that...because I have my pride. You can imagine.

YELENA: Please don't. Can't you see how distressing this is? You're putting me in an impossible situation.

VANYA: Do you think I would talk like this if I could help myself? But I can't! Since I first saw you this morning... So small and alone... I've been completely crazed. I can't eat. I can't sleep. There's only one thing, one thing I long to do. Long to do with all my heart. Take you in my arms and comfort you.

YELENA: This is agony. How can you do this to me? I'll go away. I'll go away tomorrow. I don't care any more.

VANYA: (*Stops her at the door.*) I beg you, Yelena Andreyevna. Please don't go away. You must never go away again. Please forgive me. I won't talk to you like that again. I'll cut out my tongue rather than talk to you like that again. Just look at me. Look at me with your sweet, sweet eyes. And let me kiss your hand before you go. That's all I ask.

(*YELENA slowly lifts her head and looks at VANYA. Then she lifts her hand and offers it to him. He kisses her hand lingeringly. She turns and leaves the room. VANYA stays where he is and seems a little dazed.*)

(*Softly.*) She let me kiss her hand. Let me touch her delicate skin with my lips. She didn't pull away. And the way she looked at me. So sweetly, so sweetly. Oh God, I must be dreaming... Dreaming... Dreaming. (*Holds his head while he sits down slowly.*) Oh... I'm delirious. (*Slow fade to black.*)

End of Act One.

ACT TWO

Two months later. Ten in the evening. The windows are wide open. Intense moonlight shines into the room. The only other source of light is the lamp hanging above the table. The study and the dining-room doors are closed. On the small table there is half a glass of red wine, as well as a nearly full bottle of wine. On the round table there is food on a tray. TELEGIN is softly playing a melancholy tune on his guitar. VANYA is sitting on an armchair. His head is against the back of the chair and his eyes are closed as he listens to the music. SONYA is sitting on the window seat in front of the open window, also listening.

SONYA: My head aches from this unbearable heat. It's so close. If it doesn't rain soon I don't know what I'll do.
(*TELEGIN finishes playing.*)

VANYA: Come on, my friend. Play some more! (*Little laugh.*) I don't know what it is with me. I'm in such a strange mood. Must be the room.

SONYA: You've been very strange lately uncle. That's true.

TELEGIN: When it rose... I took my poor wife to the window. I said, 'See how big and round and bright it is. And look how the birch trees are shining in the moonlight.'

VANYA: Play! Play, my friend!
(*TELEGIN plays a little louder. VANYA hums and keeps time with his hand.*)

SONYA: Don't make so much noise. You'll wake Yelena.

TELEGIN: Of course.
(*TELEGIN plays more quietly.
Short silence.*)

SONYA: I took her some supper earlier. (*Points at the supper tray on the table.*) But she hardly ate a thing.
(*Short silence.*)

VANYA: (*Gets up and walks about with his hands behind his back.*) It touches me... It really touches me...to see how brave she is. I hear her coughing, sometimes all night... Now she's too weak even to climb the stairs...and yet she never complains. (*Helps himself to food from YELENA's tray.*)

SONYA: Don't do that, Uncle. It's disgusting! Eating someone else's leftovers.

TELEGIN: (*Laughs.*) Quite right. (*He stops playing.*)

SONYA: You might even get infected.

VANYA: You should have seen how she thanked me for getting the specialist from Moscow. She thanked me with tears in her eyes. She took my hands and called me 'a dear, good man'.

SONYA: Well, you are very good to her uncle. The specialist costs the earth. I hardly know how we'll pay him.

VANYA: (*To TELEGIN.*) He's talking to Astrov now. Advising him. Astrov tells me he's very highly regarded. One of the best. I'm sure he'll suggest a wonderful cure.

SONYA: Astrov knows about all the latest methods. Really, I hardly think it was necessary. Just a ridiculous expense! (*Short silence.*)

TELEGIN: Tonight when I was walking here, I heard the birds singing in the birch trees. They always sing when the moon is so bright. I looked up at the stars and I thought: 'I'm a happy man'. I don't know why...but I am.

SONYA: What a dear man you are, godfather.

YELENA: (*Enters from the study. The top buttons of her dress are undone and her hair's down. Her cheeks seem unhealthily flushed and her eyes too bright.*) I had a peaceful little sleep. I think my fever must be down. Oh, what a relief. Those fever dreams... They're not like other dreams. Horrible. So horrible. And you keep having them...even with your eyes wide open. But I won't even think about that. (*Little laugh.*)

TELEGIN: You see Yelena Andreyevna, there was nothing to worry about. You're on the mend.
(*Short silence.*)

YELENA: Has Astrov finished talking to the specialist?

SONYA: Not yet.

YELENA: I feel a little dizzy.

SONYA: Come and sit down. You must be exhausted.

YELENA: Yes...well... I haven't had much sleep for the last few nights.

SONYA: Why don't you let Astrov give you something to let you sleep? You need to sleep.

VANYA: Sonya's right. You'll wear yourself out.

YELENA No... No... I just need to get a little fresh air. (*She leans out of the window.*)

SONYA: It's very close tonight.

YELENA: This heat is terrible. Like a weight pushing down on me. I simply can't bear the heat. It affects me very badly.

(*Short silence.*)

TELEGIN: I think I must be going. My wife will be waiting for me. This morning she started darning my socks. Imagine that.

SONYA: So she's feeling better?

TELEGIN: She's still a little confused, poor soul. Doesn't really know me. But she has a good heart. There's one thing I find quite funny...and I suppose pathetic in a way... She keeps asking me to brush her hair. She used to have long, soft hair when she was young. But now she hardly has any.

YELENA: What can they be talking about? It's been more than an hour.

VANYA: Oh, you know what doctors are like. If it's not one thing, it's another.

YELENA: Yes... Yes... (*She sits down on the window seat and passes her hand over her eyes.*)

SONYA: Come now. Be reasonable. How much longer can you go on like this? You need some rest.

YELENA: No, I can't possibly sleep. I have too many things to think about. Too many plans to make.

SONYA: Plans?

YELENA: Yes, yes. (*She gets up and starts walking about restlessly.*) You see...it's very lovely here in the country. But the heat...the mosquitoes... It's all making me much worse. All the foul, farm smells. And the flies... They sit on my eyelids when I sleep. On my lips. And so, during the day, I have to keep my windows closed. Even in this heat. Then it's really too horrible. Completely stifling in there.

SONYA: Well, I'm sorry that you feel like this. We really do our best.

YELENA: Oh, I don't mean to be... You've been so kind. Really it's meant so much to me. You can't imagine what I've been through. (*Tearfully.*) But can't you see that this place is making me very ill?

VANYA: We could put screens on the windows. I'll have it done tomorrow. No...no. I'll have it done at once. This very minute!

TELEGIN: That should do the trick.

YELENA: It's no good. It's no good. I have to leave. I have to. As soon as possible.

VANYA: To leave? Just like that? But you haven't said anything.

YELENA: I must get away as soon as possible. I won't get better until I do. You must understand.

SONYA: But you're in no fit state to travel.

TELEGIN: Yes. Listen to Sonechka. From what I understand, you are really very ill Yelena Andreyevna.

YELENA: (*Coldly.*) I know what's best for me!

SONYA: Well, you must do as you wish.

YELENA: I'm sorry. I didn't mean to speak to you like that. A few days longer. Yes, perhaps a few days longer. Until I'm stronger.

VANYA: But it's all so sudden. I thought you were coming to live in the country. You promised. That's what you wrote. To live here with us in the country. I never thought you would be leaving. You never told me. Why didn't you tell me? No-one ever tells me anything! (*Takes a swig from the wine bottle.*)

SONYA: Oh, Uncle...

VANYA: Be quiet! I'm sick and tired! Sick and tired of your nagging!

SONYA: (*Tearfully.*) There. He's starting again. (*Angrily to YELENA.*) You could have told me sooner. I have a house to run, you know.

VANYA: (*Lifting the bottle.*) What shall we drink to, Waffles my old friend? Let's drink to me! Who wanted to write...like Dostoevsky. Who wanted to know... passionate love! (*Expansive gesture.*) Many women! Hundreds of them! But who pissed away...his miserable life...his un-speak-ably drea-ry life...in this hole!

SONYA: (Covering *her ears.*) I wish you wouldn't talk like that, Uncle! It's disgusting!

TELEGIN: I really must be going...

VANYA: Yes...let's go! To hell with it!

TELEGIN: Goodnight Yelena Andreyevna. Sonechka.

YELENA: Goodnight.

SONYA: Goodnight

VANYA: For God's sake, let's go!

(*TELEGIN exits. VANYA follows him, carrying the bottle of wine.*

Short silence.)

SONYA: Can you see how unhappy he is. If he starts drinking again I don't know what I'll do! Whenever uncle is listening to you, glances after you when you leave a room, I've noticed something so tender and innocent in his look. Surely you haven't given him any hope? That would be too cruel.

YELENA: I've done nothing. I'm pleasant to him. I like him. Maybe he misunderstood. But it's not my fault. Life here is so wretched and trivial. I suppose I'm different, still quite attractive in my way. And so they get carried away. It gives them something to do, you see.

SONYA: You mean Astrov too, don't you? No, don't say anything. I can see the way he looks at you. Nothing has changed.

(*In the distance TELEGIN starts playing a melancholy tune while VANYA sings along out-of-tune.*)

VANYA: (*Singing.*) 'My dearest love, my dearest love...'

SONYA: Believe me, it doesn't matter. When he proposed to me...

VANYA: (*Singing.*) 'My love is lost to me...'

SONYA: I knew he had no romantic feelings for me. I didn't care. I was so happy. You see, I didn't know how terrible it would be...

VANYA: (*Singing.*) 'May no-one know this sorrow.'

SONYA: Never to be looked at...like that.

VANYA: (*Singing.*) 'Which touches me so closely...'

YELENA: Sonya my dear. Don't...

SONYA: What a melancholy song. (*Tearful.*) It always makes me sad (*Wipes her eyes.*) I mustn't let Astrov see me crying. (*Bitterly.*) It...irritates him. (*Short silence.*) I've been so lonely. You have no idea. I've had no-one to talk to. And even you... Ever since you arrived you've been avoiding me. Admit it. But then...I suppose I'm not very interesting.

(*The lamp flickers.*)

YELENA: That's not true. I've just had so much on my mind. (*Looking up.*) The lamp is flickering.

SONYA: I remember the talks we used to have. How we told each other everything. Once I asked you if you were happy with my father, or if he was too old for you. And you said he was. And that you wished you'd married a younger man. How I admired your honesty.

YELENA: What a strange girl you are. (*Sits down next to her on the sofa.*) What a good, kind girl. (*Touches her hair.*)

SONYA: You once told me I had lovely hair. (*Puts her head on YELENA's shoulder.*) Oh... I suddenly feel so peaceful. (*Silence. YELENA strokes her hair.*)

(*Inhales deeply.*) I remember the smell of your perfume. Like wild flowers.

(*The lamp flickers.*)

(*Looking up.*) I must have forgotten to fill it this morning. (*YELENA moans softly.*)

What is it?

YELENA: On stifling hot nights like these – I've always had the strangest feeling. Ever since I can remember.

SONYA: What kind of feeling?

(*The lamp starts flickering.*)

YELENA: I don't know where it comes from. From deep inside me...or from all around me...

SONYA: I simply can't bear hot nights. I know what you mean.

VANYA: It's really like the strangest yearning. It makes my throat swell... (*Touching her throat.*) and ache almost unbearably.
(*The lamp goes down.*)

YELENA: Look, the lamp is going down.
(*The lamp goes out.*)
Now it's gone right out. I'm afraid of the dark.

SONYA: There's a candelabra in the dining-room. I'll get it. (*Gets up and moves towards the dining-room.*)

YELENA: I've always been afraid of the dark. I keep a candle burning next to my bed all night. But sometimes it goes out.
(*TELEGIN's playing and VANYA's singing can be heard again. But now much further away – the words of the song cannot be distinguished.*
SONYA goes into the dining-room.)
(*Calling after her.*) Whenever I wake up in the dark, I close my eyes and wait...just wait. I'm scared to open my eyes, to lift my head. It's an...unreasoning, animal fear. Why I'm so scared... I don't have the faintest idea.
(*SONYA re-enters with the candelabra.*)
And then it always sounds to me as if someone is groaning or laughing somewhere very close to me. Strange...

SONYA: When I wake up at night, I always feel like eating an apple or an orange.
(*They laugh softly.*)

YELENA: (*Seeing the glass of wine on the small table.*) What's this?

SONYA: Astrov was having some wine earlier on.

YELENA: (*Picks up the glass.*) I might as well have some. (*Drinks.*) I don't know... I feel so strange tonight. (*Puts the glass down.*)

SONYA: Poor Astrov. He works too hard. It's the Cholera epidemic. And then I often feel...somehow so angry with him. I'm always nagging him. But then I can't seem to help it.

YELENA: I should go and lie down. I feel a little flushed. (*Gets up.*)

SONYA: Of course. I suppose...I've been tiring you.
(*Gets up.*)

YELENA: It's just that I don't want to get another fever.
It's too awful to think about. (*She goes into the study.*)

SONYA: (*Stands in the study door softly.*) I could sit with you.
I'll be very quiet. I'll bring my knitting.

YELENA: (*Comes to the door softly.*) I'm quite happy to be
alone. In fact I prefer it.

SONYA: Well, then...(*Turns away.*)

YELENA: Not that I'm not grateful, you understand.

SONYA: You don't want my company. You should be honest
about it! You think I'm dull...and stupid
(*SONYA goes to the window. The music and singing fades
away completely.*)

YELENA: I can't argue with you. I'm too tired. When
Astrov comes in you must let me know at once, my dear.
(*She closes the study door.*)
(*SONYA leans out of the window. She suddenly starts giving
gasping sobs.*)

ASTROV: (*Entering. Irritable.*) Why the hell is it so dark in
here? I can't see a thing! For God's sake, don't tell me
you're crying again.

SONYA: (*Turning from the window.*) Why do you speak to
me like this? I can't bear it!

ASTROV: For God's sake, what's the matter now?

SONYA: You don't even see me any more. Our life together
is nothing. Nothing. I see it all now. It's so senseless. So
ridiculous. I've prayed. How I've prayed for the Lord to
give me strength. I simply can't bear it any longer.

NANNY: (*Voice off.*) Sonya! Sonya!

ASTROV: Can't you understand that this is the worst
possible time? What's suddenly possessed you?

SONYA: Of course. You never have time for me, do you?
No one ever has time for me!

YELENA: (*Enters. To ASTROV.*) I heard your voice...

NANNY: (*Off.*) Sonya!

SONYA: (*Tearful.*) Yes Nanny! I'm coming! (*Storms out.*)
(*Short silence.*)

YELENA: Has the doctor left?

ASTROV: Yes. He's catching the midnight train to Moscow.

YELENA: (*Stands in front of the window.*) Oh...at last there's a breeze. (*Little laugh.*) And just look at the moon. It's so huge. It's almost frightening. (*Leans out a little.*) Lovely. (*Turns around.*) I hope you don't mind. I drank some of your wine. (*Laugh.*) I should never drink wine in the heat. It makes my pulse race.

(*Short silence.*)

Why is Sonya so upset? Is it something you told her about me?

ASTROV: No. Of course not. Just a little domestic squabble.

YELENA: I see.

(*Short silence. ASTROV watches her.*)

(*Softly.*) Don't. Don't look at me like that.

(*ASTROV turns his head away.*

Short silence.)

ASTROV: You should let me give you something to calm your nerves.

YELENA: (*Goes into the dining-room. Calls from there.*) Well, you might as well tell me what the doctor said. How long will it be? When will I be well enough to travel? (*Draws a finger over the keys of the piano.*)

ASTROV: Travel? My dear Yelena Andreyevna... You have to understand!

YELENA: (*Stands in the door.*) I must get away from this place as soon as possible. Surely that's obvious.

ASTROV: (*Sits on the couch.*) Please come and sit here next to me. I need to talk to you.

YELENA: A week? Two weeks? Even longer? Oh, that would be almost intolerable. There's so much space here. So much endless space. And... I'm being suffocated. How can one explain that? From the moment I stepped off the train... I wanted to get away. Get away and never come back. You must think me very ungrateful. After all you've done. But I can't help it. I simply can't.

ASTROV: Yelena. Listen to me. The specialist has just confirmed what I think. You're very ill indeed. You've certainly not well enough to travel.

YELENA: I've had a setback, I know. But I've had many
haemorrhages and completely recovered.
(*VANYA can be heard approaching. He is singing rather
drunkenly.*)

ASTROV: Yelena, I'm very sorry. (*He gets up and goes to her.*)
But I have to tell you...as your doctor I can simply not
allow you to go. You would be risking your life.

YELENA: (*Calm.*) You're quite wrong, of course.

ASTROV: Please...

YELENA: (*Calmly.*) You don't know me. You know nothing
about me. You don't know what strength I have...

VANYA: (*Off. Singing.*) 'My dearest love, my dearest love...'

ASTROV: Yelena... (*Touches her arm.*)

YELENA: Don't touch me! Keep away from me!

VANYA: (*Enters singing. He leans against the doorframe,
conducting with one hand.*) 'My love is lost to me... May
no one know this sorrow, which touches me...'

YELENA: (*Interrupting him.*) Thank God you're here Ivan
Petrovich. Please... I need you to help me.

VANYA: But of course. (*Sarcastic.*) Anything. (*Bows.*)
Anything.

YELENA: (*Speaking very fast.*) You're such a good, kind man.
Such a good, kind man. Such a friend. Dear kind Ivan
Petrovich. I want to ask you, to beg for my allowance.
Not just for this month, but for a few months in advance.

VANYA: (*Angrily.*) I don't understand anything any more!
Nothing makes sense any more! And I don't even care.
(*Sings loudly and moves to the study.*)

YELENA: (*Following him.*) I know it's a great deal to ask,
but I'm quite desperate you see. Surely you can see that.
You must understand that I have to go away. I have to go
away. Or else...something terrible will happen. I know it.
I feel it... (*Touches her chest.*) right here.

VANYA: Well go away then! Go away! Who's stopping you?

ASTROV: It's out of the question. I've told her that. (*Opens
his bag. Starts mixing something into the wine left in the glass.
VANYA sits down.*)

YELENA: (*Weeping and trying to hold VANYA back.*) Please,
please. I know what I have to do. I must get back to

Germany. To the Black Forest. The sweet air. And then I'll get well again. I know it. Please dear Ivan Petrovich. (*Coughs.*)

ASTROV: Yelena, I want you to drink this. (*Holds out the wine glass.*) If you want your strength back...you must do as I tell you.

YELENA: I don't want it.

ASTROV: Drink it. It'll make you feel better. You'll see. (*YELENA drinks almost without being aware of what she is doing.*)

VANYA: But...where am I supposed to get the money? Where am I supposed to get it? I don't really know what's happening. I'm completely confused. Bloody women!

YELENA: (*Desperately.*) I'll do anything. Anything.

VANYA: Oh, just leave me alone. If you hate us and if you hate this place, then you must go and never come back!

YELENA: Please. Please listen to me. I beg you.

VANYA: (*Shaking her off.*) Let go of me!

YELENA: (*Desperately.*) All those letters you wrote... Asking me. Imploring me. Well then Ivan Petrovich... I'll marry you. Yes, yes I will. As soon as I'm better. If only you'll help me now!

VANYA: For God's sake Yelena Andreyevna! How can you behave like a woman of that kind! It's simply... preposterous. I can't believe it! How can you do something like this?

ASTROV: She doesn't know what she's saying. She's feverish.

YELENA: I know precisely! I don't want to die here. Here...in this miserable place. I want to live! To live! (*To VANYA.*) But what would you know about living? With your tepid, sentimental yearnings. How you sicken me!

ASTROV: Yelena! For God's sake!

YELENA: Don't look at me! (*Goes towards the study door. Turns at the door, almost snarling.*) Keep away from me! (*Exits and slams the door behind her.*) (*Silence.*)

VANYA: Good God, has this really happened? It seems more like…a horrible nightmare. For years I've worshipped her… Idealised her. But she's no better than a common whore.
(*Far off howling of dogs. The dogs continue to howl from time to time until otherwise indicated in the text.*)

ASTROV: Come now, old friend. I can understand how you feel.

VANYA: (*Slowly shaking his head.*) No, no you can't. You can't begin to understand. Oh God, just listen to those vile brutes! Sometimes they howl all night! (*Puts his hands over his ears.*) I don't want to hear them. I can't bear it! I want them to be quiet!

ASTROV: Don't upset yourself. I'll close the window.
(*He closes the window.*)

VANYA: It's no use. That eerie, terrible sound. It goes right through me. The only way to shut them up, would be to shoot them. Yes, I'm going to get my gun right now and shoot them. (*Weeps.*)

SONYA: (*Puts her head around the door.*) I have something to say to Astrov. I might as well say it in front of you, Uncle. It hardly matters. (*To ASTROV.*) I've taken your things to the room at the end of the passage.

VANYA: But what's happening?

SONYA: I want you to know Uncle… It's all over between Astrov and me! All over! (*Tearfully.*) Those dogs are driving me crazy! (*She disappears again.*)

VANYA: But what's happening tonight? All hell is breaking loose.

ASTROV: Oh, it'll blow over. You know women.
(*Short silence.*)
In many ways she's an unfortunate woman. She's hardly had much of a life.

VANYA: Well, this life of ours… It's not much to speak of either.

ASTROV: Married to Sonya's father, the professor. A woman like that. To be kissed by those bloodless lips. It used to make me shudder.

VANYA: I could never understand it.

ASTROV: She thought he was a fine man. A learned man. That he would open new worlds for her. Instead of course...

(*The dogs stop howling.*)

VANYA: Yes... Yes. It was the same with my late sister. She was so warm and generous, and he killed her! He killed her with his cold-blooded egotism! I told Yelena Andreyevna she was wasting herself on him. That she was an exquisite creature. That she had mermaid's blood in her veins.

ASTROV: Mermaid's blood. (*Laughs.*) That's true...

VANYA: But still. To offer herself to me like that. It was vile. Completely vile.

ASTROV: In some sense of course you're right...

YELENA: (*Appears in the study door. She is unsteady on her feet.*) Astrov...please help me. (*She walks unsteadily into the room.*) I feel so strange... I don't know what's happening to me...

(*ASTROV gets up and takes her arm.*)

I'm so dizzy... So dizzy... My head seems to be floating away from me.

VANYA: What's wrong with her?

ASTROV: (*To YELENA.*) Don't be alarmed. Come and sit down here. (*Leads her to the couch.*) You're very drowsy, that's all. (*YELENA sits.*) Earlier I gave you something to make you sleep.

YELENA: Sleep? I don't want to sleep. (*Gets up unsteadily.*)

ASTROV: You really need to get some rest.

YELENA: I have to stay awake... Have to stay awake. Have to...

ASTROV: Come now. Don't fight it. It will only make you feel worse.

YELENA: I have to leave you see... Can't stay. (*Leans against the table.*)

ASTROV: When you wake up, you'll feel much better.

YELENA: (*Points to the hall door.*) I have to go through that door... Across the hall... Down the steps...into the garden.

ASTROV: Come now. You should lie down. (*He takes her arm.*)

YELENA: (*Shrugs him off.*) And down the thin avenue of white birch trees. (*Closes her eyes. Sways.*) I can't breathe...

ASTROV: You need some air. Come over to the window. (*ASTROV leads her to the window.*)

YELENA: There are shadows everywhere...

ASTROV: Sit down here for a minute. (*He pushes her gently onto the window seat.*) And I'll open the window. (*He opens the window.*) Is that better?

YELENA: Ah... (*Leans out of the window. Extends her arms and moves them slowly.*) Lovely...cool...air. (*Gets up. Her arms drop slowly.*) I mustn't sleep...I mustn't... (*Sways.*) I'm not here any more... I'm gone...gone...gone. (*ASTROV catches her as she falls and lowers her onto the floor. Stands looking down at her. Silence. ASTROV and VANYA watch as she falls asleep.*)

VANYA: To drug her like this. It doesn't seem right.

ASTROV: Did you want her to go on exhausting herself? It could have been quite fatal.

VANYA: But to see her like this. So helpless. It's dreadful. Quite dreadful. (*Holds out his hands.*) Just look at my hands. Can you see how they're trembling?

ASTROV: I'm a doctor of course. So I've become quite used to this kind of thing. And worse. Much worse. For instance...death is often not very pleasant. And yet...I've often thought how a lovely woman, in her death agonies, sometimes seems to be in the transports of erotic pleasure. (*Little laugh.*) I don't believe anyone else has ever remarked on that before. (*Now YELENA's asleep, her face looks very drawn and even plain.*)

VANYA: Poor creature. I can hardly bear to look at her.

ASTROV: She is certainly to be pitied.

VANYA: I'm sorry for her. I really am... But after what happened earlier... After what she said to me...I can't possibly stay under the same roof with her. I'll have to go and stay with Telegin and his hag until she's well enough to leave.

ASTROV: I don't think that's a good idea.

VANYA: Why not?

ASTROV: She won't be well enough to leave for quite some time. I don't think she'll ever be quite well again. In fact, if we don't take the utmost care of her, she might not even last out the month.

VANYA: Good God. Is it as bad as that?

ASTROV: I'm afraid so.

VANYA: That's dreadful. Dreadful.

ASTROV: That's why I must ask you (*He takes off YELENA's shoe.*) to find it in your heart to forget what happened. (*Takes off her other shoe.*) To put it all behind you. She needs us now. I mean, where will she go? (*He undoes her top buttons.*) She has no family as you know. If we send her away – let me speak quite plainly – we would be sending her to her death.

VANYA: But she wants to leave. She hates this place! You heard what she said!

ASTROV: When the fever goes down, I'll speak to her. Explain everything. Believe me, she'll see reason. She has no choice.

VANYA: Well...I suppose...in that case. (*Looks down at her.*) Yes...Yes...I see what you mean. After all, in a way, she's our responsibility.

ASTROV: Quite.

(*A short silence as the two men look at YELENA.*)

VANYA: To stay here with us...To live with us. Yes...yes ...I see what you mean.

ASTROV: I believe it's the right thing to do.

VANYA: To keep her here... To keep her here. We must be kind. You're quite right. My dear friend, my dear Astrov, you really are a wise man. A generous man. Yes, I can see it quite clearly now. There's nothing else to do. After all, she's just a poor, weak creature. My dear friend...Let me embrace you. (*He embraces ASTROV.*) I feel so moved... So moved. So grateful to you. (*Short silence.*) What a strange night this is. What a terrible...and wonderful night. I...must go outside. Yes...I'll sit in the garden... Look at the moon. I can't possibly sleep tonight.

ASTROV: And I'll stay with her in case she needs me.

VANYA: Quite right...quite right...
*(He wipes his eyes, then turns and goes through the hall door.
ASTROV remains motionless, looking down at YELENA.
After a time VANYA can be heard humming in the garden.
ASTROV bends down and clumsily lifts YELENA. He
stumbles to the bedroom carrying her as the lights slowly fade
to black.)*

End of Act Two.

ACT THREE

Three months later. Wooden 'inner shutters' have been put on the windows as a protection against the cold. The process has been begun but not completed and there are shutters on only some of the windows. It is nine in the evening. The lamp above the table is lit. Candlelight can be seen through the open doors of the study, hall and the dining-room; dimly from the study and the hall and brighter from the dining-room. There are roses arranged on the small table, on the table and on the sideboard. There are slightly over-bright new pillows on the couch. There is a sewing basket on the small table. The sound of very soft rain. When the lights go up, astrov can be seen sitting at the table. He seems to be tensely listening. After a while, voices can be heard in the hall.

SONYA: (*Off.*) Now it's so cold. You'll hardly believe me...
 (*YELENA enters with SONYA behind her. YELENA is dressed in a severe dark green coat, black kid-leather gloves and a small black hat with a short veil.*)
 ...but last week it was so warm that we sat on the verandah every evening.

ASTROV: (*Getting up.*) Well, Yelena Andreyevna. Back at last.

YELENA: As you see.

SONYA: And with all this rain we've been getting, we're afraid that the hay will rot. (*Looking back into the hall.*) Oh, Uncle, you should close an umbrella before you come into the house. You know how unlucky it is.

VANYA: (*Entering.*) The servants were going to take your luggage to my room. I told them we weren't married yet. That they would have to wait. (*Laughs.*)

YELENA: Yes.

VANYA: Sometimes I can hardly believe it.

SONYA: I prepared a light supper for you.

VANYA: What a kind girl you are.

SONYA: (*To YELENA.*) You're still wearing your hat.

YELENA: All these flowers. Quite suffocating.

SONYA: I'm sorry you don't like them.

YELENA: It's not that. They're lovely. Really lovely.

TELEGIN: (*Entering.*) Well, the luggage has been taken care of.

VANYA: Thank you my dear Waffles.

SONYA: I picked all the last roses. To welcome you back.

VANYA: Lovely autumn roses.

ASTROV: Yes... It's September already. However shall we get through the winter here?

SONYA: Oh, there's a great deal to do. A great deal to keep us busy. You'll see.

YELENA: Yes.

SONYA: (*To TELEGIN.*) Godfather dear, if I've asked you once, I've asked you a hundred times to wipe your feet before you come into the house. There's mud all over the carpet.

TELEGIN: I'm very sorry. (*Looks down at his feet.*)
(*Short silence.*)

VANYA: And what do you think of the pillows? Sonechka embroidered them herself.

YELENA: Everything looks very nice.

SONYA: You should really take off your hat.

YELENA: Yes... (*Takes off her hat and puts it on the table.*)

SONYA: What a beautiful hatpin. Mother-of-pearl. (*Sits at the table.*)

VANYA: I bought it for her as an engagement present at one of those posh Moscow shops.

SONYA: I'm afraid you've been extravagant, Uncle. (*Tearfully.*) And you know quite well that we don't have any money.

TELEGIN: Imagine, you've been all the way to Germany, Yelena Andreyevna. All the places and the people you must have seen. Even bathing in a hot spring.

SONYA: And now you'll have to become used to our dull faces again. Poor Yelena.

TELEGIN: Imagine! I've spent my whole miserable life in this place. Once, when I was young, I went on a journey. Had a few adventures. But I can hardly remember anything about that now. (*Laughs.*)

SONYA: I've only been to Kharkov. But that was for father's funeral. And I was too sad to see anything... It rained and snowed at father's funeral. I remember that.

(*Short silence.*)

VANYA: Oh, and I had my mother's engagement ring made smaller. And now it fits perfectly. Show them, Lienochka. (*YELENA takes off her glove and extends her hand.*)

SONYA: (*Going closer.*) It looks very nice.

ASTROV: Let me see. (*He goes to her. Touches her fingers lightly.*) Lovely.

TELEGIN: Poor Maria Vasilyevna. It makes me think of her. I can still see that ring on her finger. She never took it off.

(*YELENA moves to the window.*)

NANNY: (*Off.*) Sonya! Sonya!

SONYA: Oh, I've forgotten about Nanna Marina. I promised to tell her the moment you arrived. She's been so terribly worried. She thought you'd fallen off the edge of the world.

(*SONYA exits through the hall door.*)

VANYA: Poor old Nanny. How I should hate to be blind. Darkness. Always darkness. I would rather not live. When I met Yelena at the station in Moscow, we ran into one of her old music professors. He said she'd been his most brilliant pupil. Quite brilliant. He had very high hopes for her.

ASTROV: You've been far too modest, Yelena Andreyevna. Now you'll have to play for us.

SONYA: In your letters you said you played every day at the sanatorium.

YELENA: The weather was so bad...I had nothing else to do.

ASTROV: It was kind of you...to write so dutifully.

VANYA: (*Brightly.*) Yes. Every week. I have all your letters in my desk.

SONYA: (*Entering.*) Nanny is so excited. I hope you've brought her a present from Moscow Uncle. She said you promised to.

VANYA: Of course I did. A few trinkets to amuse her.

ASTROV: And did you see any of your other old acquaintances, Yelena Andreyevna?

YELENA: No. No-one.

(*SONYA whispers something in VANYA's ear.*)

VANYA: (*Too loudly.*) I really think we should eat something! Sonechka has made something light.

YELENA: (*Still looking out.*) No thank you. I'm not hungry.

ASTROV: And how are you feeling Yelena Andreyevna?

YELENA: (*Still looking out.*) Better. Much better. (*Little laugh.*) I've never felt better in my life.
(*Short silence.*)

TELEGIN: Well, I'd better be going. I'll come again tomorrow.

NANNY: Sonya!

SONYA: Uncle, you should really go and see Nanny. She's so impatient that I'm afraid she'll fall out of bed. (*Laughs.*)

VANYA: Well yes, let me go at once.

TELEGIN: Goodbye Ivan Petrovich. Goodbye Yelena Andreyevna. How wonderful to have you back. Now... everything is as it should be.

YELENA: Goodbye.

VANYA: Goodbye Waffles. (*To YELENA.*) I'm just going to see old Nanny.
(*TELEGIN exits to the hall.*)
Don't you want to come with me?

YELENA: Not now.

VANYA: I won't be long. (*Exits to the hall.*)

SONYA: And I'll go and get the supper ready. (*To YELENA.*) Very light. Nothing difficult to digest. You can try, at least.
(*SONYA exits to hall.*)
(*Short silence.*)

ASTROV: Can I get you something to drink?

YELENA: Brandy. Please.
(*ASTROV exits to the dining-room. YELENA turns away from the window and sits down.*)

ASTROV: (*Calling from the dining-room.*) Ivan looks so well! It's really quite disgusting! (*Laughs.*)
(*YELENA sits very quietly and looks down at her hands.*)
(*Calling.*) And as for me... The thought that I'll be seeing you every day has done wonders for me! (*Enters with two glasses of brandy. Gives one to YELENA.*)

Seems to make it all more bearable. The squalor, the epidemics, the suppurating sores, the death agonies. (*Raising his glass.*) Well then, welcome home.

YELENA: Yes. Here I am. (*Little laugh.*) Better, I suppose than dying in abject poverty. That has somehow never appealed to me. (*Drinks.*)

ASTROV: That's hardly fair. We didn't want to cut off your allowance, but there was nothing else to do. It's also been very hard on us you know. We've had to mortgage the farm almost to the hilt.

YELENA: Yes. Three months at a spa costs the earth. You don't have to tell me that again. And I'm grateful of course. Deeply grateful. But when I wanted to live so desperately... Well...you see... This is not really what I meant. (*Laughs.*) All I can hope for now is that Vanya and Sonya...will kill me with kindness. (*Drinks.*)

ASTROV: You're talking nonsense. Absolute nonsense. (*Short silence.*)
Yes. I really have a new lease on life. I've started wearing my hair quite fashionably.

YELENA: I noticed.

ASTROV: I've even developed a strangely tender affection for Sonya. It's a kind of gratitude I think. Because of her I belong to this family. Irrevocably. (*Laughs.*) And now you can never get rid of me. You'll see how much happier she seems. So, you see, you've done wonders for us all.
(*TELEGIN appears in the hall door. He is dressed in a long coat and a strange fur cap.*)

YELENA: You gave me such a fright! I didn't recognise you in those clothes.

TELEGIN: I've just come for a moment, that's why I didn't take my outside clothes off in the hall. I hope you'll forgive me, Yelena Andreyevna.

YELENA: Of course.

TELEGIN: I was halfway home when I remembered that I'd forgotten to thank you Yelena Andreyevna. For the trunk of clothes you're sending my poor wife.

YELENA: It's nothing. They're not suitable for me any more, that's all. I have to wear simple clothes now that I'm going to be a country wife.

TELEGIN: It will make her very happy. I meant to thank you before. But I'm getting so absent-minded these days. Well... I'll say goodnight then.

YELENA: Goodnight.

(*TELEGIN exits.*)

ASTROV: As I've said. (*Laughs.*) You bring happiness to us all. Even that old hag.

(*Short silence.*)

YELENA: Do you know that I envy that old woman?

TELEGIN: What? (*Laughs.*) Telegin's mad wife?

YELENA: She knew a passion that drove her to madness. And I've hardly lived at all. Day and night the thought that my life has been hopelessly wasted weighs on me like a nightmare.

TELEGIN: She's hardly been driven mad by passion. (*Laughs.*) She's suffering from senile dementia. Really Yelena Andreyevna, you've been reading too many novels.

YELENA: Yes. Perhaps you're right.

ASTROV: We're just ordinary people...living futile, wretched lives like everyone else. Take me for instance. The whole afternoon I spent with a sick child in a labourers cottage. Filth, stench, smoke. Even pigs. But having you here can somehow make us forget it. So, you see. We need you. (*Little laugh.*) To keep us alive.

YELENA: (*Softly.*) And you used to call *me* a vampire!

ASTROV: I remember. And a bird of prey. And a wild, furry animal. (*Laughs.*) Merely terms of endearment. (*Short silence.*) I keep thinking about us living under the same roof. Trapped for a long winter in this house. Even in summer. Far from town. Never seeing anyone else. (*Little laugh.*) You know very well that we're not like them. That we're two of a kind.

YELENA: Never. I would rather die.

ASTROV: People say that, but they never mean it.

VANYA: (*Entering.*) Poor old Nanny. Blind as a bat. Fancy that. She is really anxious to see you Lienochka. I promised that you would come to her at once.

YELENA: She doesn't even like me. You know that.

VANYA: Nonsense. That's not true.

YELENA: The looks she used to give me. She thought
I wasn't good enough for her precious professor.

VANYA: Oh, that's all in the past. Come on, my dear.
I promised.

YELENA: Oh, must I go into that little room? It smells of
stale urine. I can't bear it!

ASTROV: (*Laughs.*) It is rather dreadful.

VANYA: Don't be unkind. I promised her. She's waiting for
you, dear.

YELENA: Well, then I suppose I have no choice. (*Exits.*)
(*Short silence.*)

VANYA: She behaves so oddly at times. And she says the
strangest things. To tell you the truth, it worries me. By
the way. She gave me a letter from the doctor at the
sanatorium. Please read it and tell me what it says. (*Takes
an envelope out of his pocket and gives it to ASTROV.*)

ASTROV: (*Studying the letter.*) You certainly seem very well.

VANYA: Well, I can tell you, my friend…that sometimes I'm
actually happy. I can hardly believe it. And I never have a
sleepless night. (*Laughs.*) In fact, I sleep like a baby. You
see… It's the thought of having a sweet, tender creature in
my care. I feel I have something to live for now.

ASTROV: (*Still reading the letter.*) We all need that.
(*Short silence.*)

VANYA: I've been thinking… Well… Yelena Andreyevna
isn't used to our quiet way of life. We should make
things a little more sociable for her.

ASTROV: What do you mean?

VANYA: Invite the local gentry.

ASTROV: That motley lot!

VANYA: Arrange picnics, dinner-parties, musical evenings.
That sort of thing. Dancing. What does it say?

ASTROV: The doctor says there has been some improvement,
but not as much as he'd hoped.

VANYA: Well…we'll just have to take good care of her,
that's all.

ASTROV: We will. We will. And I'll examine her regularly.
(*Short silence.*)

VANYA: So. What do you think?

ASTROV: I'm afraid I don't think it would be wise.

VANYA: But why ever not? God knows, we could all do with a bit of life around here.

ASTROV: Well...with her medical history...her nature... It could excite her in quite the wrong way. And that would be very bad for her health.

VANYA: I see...

(*ASTROV and VANYA look at each other.*)

ASTROV: I would suggest...that she should live here quietly. Where we can always keep an eye on her.

(*Short silence. ASTROV and VANYA look at each other.*)

VANYA: Keep her safe.

ASTROV: Precisely.

VANYA: Yes. Yes. I believe you're right.

ASTROV: And after a while she'll get used to it. You'll see. One gets used to anything. Look at us. How used we are to this tedium which is like a strange sort of sadness.

SONYA: (*Entering with a large, heavy laden tray. She is wearing a frilly pinafore.*) The food's ready!

VANYA: (*Getting up.*) Let me take that.

SONYA: Thank you Uncle dear.

VANYA: (*Going towards the dining room.*) You must join us...

ASTROV: Thank you, I will. I quite feel like a snack.

SONYA: (*Following VANYA.*) He hardly touched his dinner tonight. Careful Uncle. I've used our best china. But I had to sell the silver.

(*VANYA pretends to stumble.*)

Oh Uncle, how silly you are. You gave me such a fright.

(*VANYA exits.*)

(*Calling after him.*) Where's Yelena?

VANYA: (*Off.*) Talking to old Marina.

SONYA: (*Turns at the door.*) Mikhail please go and call her. She really should have something to eat.

(*YELENA appears in the hall door.*)

ASTROV: Speak of the devil.

VANYA: (*Off. Calling.*) Where should I put it?

SONYA: Anywhere on the table! Come now. Have a little something.

YELENA: No, thank you. I'm not hungry.

SONYA: Please. It'll do you good.

YELENA: I don't want anything!

(*Short silence. SONYA turns away and then moves quickly to the dining room. Short silence.*)

ASTROV: And so...what did you talk to old Marina about?

YELENA: When I sat in that narrow, dank little room without even a candle... The only light from the small, blue icon lamp... I suddenly felt as if I were in a cave under the sea.

SONYA: (*Appears in the doorway, peevish.*) Mikhail, Uncle is expecting you to join him.

ASTROV: Of course. (*He goes to SONYA and whispers in her ear. Then he exits.*)

SONYA: (*After a short silence.*) Well now we can have a talk. Just the two of us. (*Short silence.*) Can I come and sit next to you?

YELENA: Of course.

(*SONYA sits next to YELENA.*)

SONYA: You're still wearing your coat. Oh well...

(*Short silence.*)

To think that you're going to be my aunt. (*Little laugh.*)

YELENA: Well, it's better than being your wicked stepmother.

(*Short silence.*)

Sonya... I didn't mean to speak to you unkindly.

(*Silence. Laughter from the dining-room.*)

SONYA: Listen to them. I think they might be getting a little drunk. But we mustn't scold them tonight.

YELENA: Oh, for God's sake Sonya, won't you take off that ridiculous thing. It makes you look so odd. As though I'm having some strange dream.

SONYA: How silly. I quite forgot about it.

(*She takes the pinafore off. Short silence.*)

I'm so happy that you're back. I can hardly tell you. I'm so lonely without you.

YELENA: How quiet it is outside. Not a single sound.

(*Getting up.*) I'm very tired. You must excuse me. I think I should get some sleep.

SONYA: Oh, please don't go yet. There's something I must tell you. I could hardly wait to tell you.

YELENA: What is it?

SONYA: Come and sit down first.

(*YELENA sits down.*)

I'm so happy. I never thought I would say that again. I'm so happy that I'm almost afraid to tell you. You have no idea how kind Astrov has been to me lately... But that's not it... Yelena... (*She takes YELENA's hands.*) there's going to be a new life in this house. If God wills it of course. A tender new life.

YELENA: Oh Sonya, I'm so glad. (*Embracing her.*) I'm so glad for you.

SONYA: Maybe this will bring us closer together. You see, I still love him. I love him so hopelessly.

(*ASTROV appears in the dining-room door. A big, white napkin is tucked into his collar and he holds a carving knife. His lips are a deep red from the wine.*)

ASTROV: Sonya, your uncle asks if you can get him some pickles.

SONYA: My goodness, I forgot the pickles. (*Getting up.*) What am I thinking of. (*Hurries out to the hall.*)

(*VANYA's voice from the dining-room.*)

VANYA: Come and eat something Lienochka. It's really delicious!

ASTROV: (*Still standing in the door. Quietly.*) Yes. Do.

YELENA: (*Quietly.*) I don't want anything.

ASTROV: (*Turning his head and calling to VANYA.*) She doesn't want anything! (*To YELENA.*) You don't want to wake up with a ravenous appetite at midnight.

VANYA: (*Off. Calling.*) No. You don't want to do that!

(*SONYA rushes on with the pickle jar and gives it to ASTROV.*)

SONYA: There you are.

ASTROV: Many thanks. (*Exits and closes the door.*)

SONYA: There's a dreadful draft. (*Closes the hall door.*)

YELENA: Why do they always eat so much? My God, it makes me feel quite ill.

SONYA: (*Sitting down.*) And I want you to help me. There's still so much sewing and knitting to be done. Of course, I would love you to be the godmother.

(*A burst of laughter from the dining room.*)

And I have something else to ask you. Something very special. If it's a girl, I would very much like to call her after you.

YELENA: (*Slowly.*) Me? Well... I don't know what to say. One usually only names a child after the dead.

SONYA: How can you say that? You're upsetting me. I shouldn't be upset. (*Tearfully.*) It's not good for me.

YELENA: (*Stilted. Without touching SONYA.*) Don't weep. Please. I can't bear it.

SONYA: You've always been so selfish. You don't care about anyone else's feelings. And couldn't you at last have eaten something. I...went to so much trouble. I've been cooking all day. My legs are aching. But what do you care!

(*VANYA and ASTROV enter.*)

VANYA: (*To ASTROV.*) As a boy and a youth, I was terrified of hall-porters and theatre ushers for some reason, and the terror is with me to this day. Now, isn't that ridiculous?

(*VANYA and ASTROV laugh.*)

That was delicious Sonechka. Just what I needed.

SONYA: (*Smiling a little too brightly. Going to ASTROV.*) Mikhail dear, you have a gravy stain on your collar. (*Touching his collar.*)

VANYA: Well, and what have the two of you been gossiping about?

(*They all look at YELENA who is distracted and seems to be listening to something they can't hear.*)

Well, well, it's getting late. I think it's bedtime.

SONYA: Uncle, I'm sorry to bother you so late, but I need you to look at the account book.

VANYA: Now? Can't it wait?

SONYA: The coal merchant is coming in the morning...and I think I've muddled things up. It won't take very long.

VANYA: (*Jovial.*) Oh, very well. Very well.

ASTROV: (*Going to the study.*) Then I might as well work on my maps.

YELENA: Maps?

ASTROV: Yes, yes. (*Exits. Calling from the study.*) I'm
drawing maps again! I remember how they used to bore
you! Now it's not forests but the spread of Cholera!
(*Coming out of the study with a rolled up map.*) Yelena
Andreyevna was always very kind. (*Laughs.*) She'd
pretend to be interested.
(*SONYA opens the drawer of the dresser to get the account
book.*
YELENA goes to the windows.)

VANYA: You can hardly expect a woman to be interested in
maps. (*Laughs.*)

SONYA: (*Taking a pair of slippers out of the drawer.*) Oh,
Uncle, I forgot. I have a surprise for you. (*Gives him his
slippers.*) See. I embroidered a daisy over that hole in the
toe.

VANYA: Just look at that. (*Taking off his boots.*) What a clever
girl you are Sonechka. You're a lucky man Astrov. I hope
you know it.
(*YELENA presses her face against the glass.*)

ASTROV: I do. (*Opening his map on the table.*)

VANYA: (*Putting on his slippers.*) There. Ivan is himself again.
(*YELENA opens the curtains.*)

SONYA: Yelena dear, it is very cold. You shouldn't press
your face aginst the glass. (*Irritable.*) It's the new moon.
There's nothing to see.

YELENA: (*Looking out.*) I can see myself. There I am. Out
there. And I can see all of you around the table.

SONYA: Come now Uncle, We have work to do. (*Takes the
account book out of the drawer.*) Come now Uncle. (*To
YELENA.*) Is it still raining?

YELENA: Softly. Very softly.

VANYA: Yes... Yes. (*Opens the book on the table.*) Oh, I forgot...
The pen is dry.

ASTROV: I have a pen. But I'm using it myself.

VANYA: That's a splendid map.

ASTROV: I haven't finished it.

SONYA: (*To YELENA. Getting ink out of the cupboard.*)
Mikhail's writing is so illegible that he dictates to me.
(*Puts the ink on the table.*) He's writing a pamphlet you
see. You must fill it, Uncle dear. I don't want my fingers

dirty when I still have to do some sewing. (*To YELENA.*)
I even know what the 'Cantini Method' is. Imagine!
(*Laughs.*) A poor, silly creature like me.
(*VANYA fills the pen.*)

VANYA: (*Drawing.*) Well, it's working. That's all I can say.

SONYA: (*Sewing.*) 'Lots of enemas with tannin at forty
degrees and injections under the skin of sodium
chloride...'

VANYA: Oh, stop it. It's too horrible. (*Laughs.*)

SONYA: (*Sing-song.*) 'The injection sometimes produces
miracles but on other occasions causes a stroke which
often results in death.'

VANYA: Enough... Enough...

SONYA: (*Laughs.*) You see, I know it by heart.

VANYA: (*Looking at the book.*) Where is it? I don't know
what I'm supposed to be looking for.

SONYA: (*Pointing.*) There, Uncle. I opened it at the place.
(*Silence.*)
(*Sewing again.*) Oh, by the way, the counsellor Serbov's
wife ran off with a travelling actor and even sold her
wedding ring.

VANYA: (*Looking at the book.*) But we seem to owe him a
fortune. How could this have happened?

SONYA: I'm sorry to say, Uncle...but as you must know...
Yelena's stay at the spa has very nearly ruined us.

VANYA: Oh well. As long as my Lienochka is better.

ASTROV: (*Laughs.*) I believe it's the fashion to run off with
actors this season.
(*YELENA wanders into the dining-room.*)

VANYA: He'll have to wait that's all.

SONYA: You must tell him Uncle. You know how angry he
gets.

ASTROV: But nothing surprises me any more. I wouldn't
be surprised if people started eating rubber-bands.

VANYA: Yes, he really is an unpleasant fellow.
(*Pause. They suddenly realise that YELENA wandered into
the dining-room.*)

ASTROV: (*Calling.*) Come and join us, Yelena Andreyevna!

VANYA: (*Calling.*) Yes, we really can't do without you dear!

SONYA: It would be so nice if you could help me! I have such a lot of sewing to do!

YELENA: (*Calling from the dining-room.*) I'm afraid I can't sew! Or knit. (*Standing in the door.*) Or cook. You see, I really don't think I'm going to be of much use to you after all.

VANYA: Nonsense, my dear. A lovely creature like you. (*Laughs.*) And you can always play the piano for us.

ASTROV: Yes, you could always do that.

SONYA: Maybe you could even play for us now.

VANYA: Excellent idea, what an excellent idea. The piano has been tuned you know. It was done while we were away. But a popular tune. Something light for this time of night. (*YELENA moves about restlessly.*)

SONYA: No. Rather something restful. To make us sleep well. Mikhail has been having such awful dreams. It's because of all the suffering he sees.

VANYA: What I would really like is for you to play my favourite song. I've forgotten how it goes. No...wait...wait... (*Hums.*) De de dum. Dee dee, dum...

SONYA: Oh Uncle dear you know you can't keep a tune.

ASTROV: That's true. (*Laughs.*)

VANYA: Wait...I'm getting it. (*Sings false and loud.*) 'Everything sings, blooms and gleams with beauuuty' There!

(*SONYA and ASTROV laugh.*)

SONYA: Uncle, I'm afraid it sounds dreadful.

VANYA: Oh, nonsense. It sounds perfectly good to me. If you can play it, I'll even sing along.

SONYA: (*Laughs.*) Oh, please say you can't play it. Please.

ASTROV: Rather play us something searing and sad. A Chopin Nocturne. Something like that.

VANYA: Oh, you and your Frenchman. (*Sings.*) 'Everything sings, blooms and gleams with beauuuty!'

SONYA: Oh stop it, stop it Uncle. Yelena, tell him to stop it.

VANYA: '...with beauuuty.'

SONYA: Oh, what a good time we're having! (*To YELENA.*) You'll see what a lovely winter we're going to have now that you're here. Time will simply fly.

VANYA: Yes...yes. In the evening we'll have games and music and singing. And when it's very cold, Yelena can play us a dance tune and we can dance and dance (*Waves his arms.*) to keep ourselves warm. (*Gets up and dances.*)

SONYA: (*Laughs.*) Oh, Uncle...

VANYA: A polka!

SONYA: You're priceless.

VANYA: A mazurka! Or gipsy dances on the table.
(*SONYA and ASTROV laugh.*
VANYA sits down..)

YELENA: You must excuse me. I'm very tired tonight.

SONYA: Please Yelena. I mean... (*Little laugh.*) Surely... It's the least you can do.

VANYA: Sonya!

YELENA: No. She's right. I'm so grateful to you. I don't know what I would have done without you. I must do anything to repay you. Of course I'll play. Of course.

VANYA: That's splendid. Isn't it splendid?

SONYA: But only if you want to. We really don't want to force you.

YELENA: Yes... I want to. To play. To sweep everything away. This dirty, tedious life.

VANYA: (*Excited.*) Yes! That's what we want!

SONYA: I'm so excited. I've waited so many years to hear you play.

VANYA: Yes. Years.

YELENA: (*Unbuttoning her coat.*) I'll perform for you.

SONYA: I can hardly believe it.

YELENA: (*Taking off her coat.*) I'll play for you every evening.

SONYA: How lovely that will be. Won't it be lovely?

VANYA: Splendid.

YELENA: And every night. (*Lightly.*) All night.

VANYA: I don't know if that's necessary dear. We need to sleep you know. (*Laughs.*)

ASTROV: To sleep. To dream... (*Laughs.*)
(*YELENA trails the coat behind her as she moves almost languidly towards the dining-room. The coat makes a sweeping sound as it slithers across the floor. Silence, as they watch her. YELENA exits.*)

VANYA: Now, don't forget to play my song!

SONYA: Ssh now, Uncle dear. Let her play what she likes.

VANYA: You're right. Imagine, she's actually going to play.

ASTROV: I told you there was nothing to worry about. She'll settle down.

SONYA: I wonder if there's enough light. (*Calling.*) Yelena dear, do you need more light?

(*No answer.*)

ASTROV: (*Whispering.*) Leave her alone. She'll tell us if she wants anything.

VANYA: (*Whispering.*) Yes, yes. That's right.

(*Short contented silence. SONYA sews, ASTROV draws and VANYA counts on his fingers.*)

SONYA: Oh... (*Weeps quietly.*)

VANYA: Why are you crying Sonechka?

SONYA: It's...because I'm so happy... So happy. Oh, dear Uncle, my dear husband... (*She puts one hand on VANYA's hand and one hand on ASTROV's.*) I suddenly feel... Oh, it's hard to explain... I suddenly feel as if our new life is just beginning... Our new...peaceful... happy life.

(*Silence. She smiles tearfully from one to the other. YELENA starts playing the short, presto movement from Scriabin's Sonata no.2 in G sharp minor. The music, tempestuous, sensuous and anarchic has been described as 'the dark agitation of the deep, deep sea'. YELENA plays the piece with passion and with brilliance. At first vanya, SONYA and ASTROV merely look puzzled and stop what they're doing. Then they look at each other with growing alarm. As the strange power of the music fills the room, they slowly turn their heads toward the dining-room where the music is coming from. VANYA, SONYA and ASTROV remain transfixed with fascinated horror as the lights slowly fade to black.*)

End of Act Three.

ACT FOUR

Three months later. Ten o'clock in the evening. YELENA's fur hat and her gloves are on the small table and a rolled up map lies on the big table. All the doors are closed. Most of the windows are shuttered against the cold. Only the two windows in the centre are unshttered. Snow is falling, very white and delicate against the darkness. The curtains are drawn and the only source of light is the lamp above the table. SONYA is sitting on the sofa, knitting a snow-white baby blanket. She is dressed in a thick padded coat. A woollen shawl covers her head and she is wearing mittens. YELENA is dressed in a coat with a fur collar and cuffs. She is looking out of the window.

YELENA: What can be keeping Astrov? It's getting so late.
> I wonder how long it takes to get to the station in a
> sleigh.
> (*She glances at SONYA. SONYA doesn't look at her. Short silence.*)
> About half an hour I suppose. At least the wind's
> dropped and its not snowing so heavily. How strange it
> is. God knows, I've seen enough snow in my life, but
> whenever I see it falling like this, I find it strange and
> unearthly.

SONYA: Poor Mikhail. He'll be frozen when he gets back.
> And then he has to go out again. I don't know why he
> insists on going with you to the station.

YELENA: Ssh. (*Listening.*) I thought I heard something.
> I must have imagined it. I've left a big trunk. I can't take
> it on the sleigh. If you could arrange for it to be sent on
> my dear, I would really be very grateful. I'll let you
> know where I am as soon as I've found a place.

SONYA: I have so much to do. I really don't know if I can
> manage that.

YELENA: Whenever you have the time. There is no hurry.

SONYA: I wish I could go away. Just go away and leave
> everything behind.

YELENA: But why would you want to do that?

SONYA: Mikhail has been so strange lately. I've even started thinking that he was going to leave me.

YELENA: You're being silly.

SONYA: Then the terrible nausea that almost never goes away... All the rain... The hay rotting...

YELENA: I really think you'd feel better if you didn't go about dressed like that.

SONYA: And what would you like me to do? Catch my death? Even now my fingers are frozen. Here. Feel them.

YELENA: No... No. I believe you.

SONYA: My circulation's never been good. Mikhail always complains about my cold feet. Even in summer. But now I'm always shivering. The house is like an ice-chest.

YELENA: Yes. Yes. Because you can't afford to heat it properly. And I know why. Ever since I've come back from Germany, you've been looking at me with those accusing eyes of yours. You've blamed me for everything. Even the weather!

SONYA: Go on then! Go on! Blame me for driving you away!

YELENA: Where is Astrov? Where is he? (*Opens the hall door and goes out.*) If I have to stay here another night, I'll go mad!
(*SONYA drops her knitting. She puts her hands over her face and starts sobbing bitterly.*)
(*Appears in the door.*) Don't... Don't... I'm sorry... (*Moves towards SONYA. Sits down on the couch next to her.*) My dear, we must forgive each other. We mustn't part like this.
(*SONYA nods.*)
Who knows if we'll ever meet again.

SONYA: Why do you say things like that?

YELENA: It's stupid of me. Of course we'll see each other. We'll see each other soon.

SONYA: I'll miss you so much... I don't know what I'll do.

YELENA: You'll be so busy, you'll hardly even think of me.

SONYA: You know that's not true.
(*Short silence.*)

YELENA: I had such a peculiar dream last night. I keep thinking about it.

SONYA: I don't like hearing about bad dreams.

YELENA: Not a bad dream exactly. Almost...peaceful.
I dreamt that I saw some horses lying in a ravine. Quite close together...

SONYA: Don't tell me any more. The slightest thing upsets me these days. You know that.

YELENA: Yes, I know. But it's given me such a sense of...foreboding. I'm afraid to leave...but I know I must.

SONYA: But why when it's so cold? You know it's not good for your health. I hope you don't mind me saying so...but you're not looking very well. And I hear you coughing at night.

YELENA: Oh, my health. I've accepted the fact that I'll always be an invalid. And then... I don't really want to grow old.

SONYA: Don't' say that. There's always hope.

YELENA: I've become a realist. Astrov taught me that.
(*Mimicking ASTROV.*) 'You simply have to be realistic.'
(*Little laugh.*
Short silence.)

SONYA: You talked very late last night.

YELENA: Yes. I suppose we did.

SONYA: Did Mikhail say anything about me?

YELENA: No. Why should he? Oh...we spoke of this and that... You know how it is.
(*Short silence.*)

SONYA: If only you could have stayed until the spring. Until my confinement.

YELENA: I wanted to be with you. But since I told your uncle that I couldn't marry him after all... Well...
I couldn't really stay.

SONYA: Poor uncle...

YELENA: Now he blames me for all his unhappiness.

SONYA: You broke his heart. Surely you can see that?

YELENA: I'm fond of him. Grateful to him. And I tried to love him. I really tried. But I couldn't. Surely I can't be blamed for that?

SONYA: No. I suppose not. But if you'd stayed a little longer...he might have made his peace with you.

YELENA: (*Getting up.*) Oh it's not only that. It's this...
restlessness that torments me... It always has... The need
to be moving... To be doing something new... Or else
I feel that life is simply passing me by... That I'm not
really living at all... That's why I've never amounted to
anything... Not in my romantic affairs... Not in my
music... Oh well... (*Laughs.*) Let's not talk about that.
(*SONYA gives a soft moan.*)
What's wrong?

SONYA: It's this terrible nausea. It's getting worse again.
It's awful. I ate a few dry biscuits a while ago, but I don't
even think I'll be able to keep them down. (*Gets up and
puts down her knitting.*) Sometimes I can't even drink a
little water. (*Moving to the hall door.*) Please call me as
soon as Mikhail comes. I want to dry his coat in front of
the fire. (*Exits to the hall.*)

YELENA: (*Calling after her.*) There won't be time for that!
It's getting very late!
(*YELENA moves about restlessly. Then she notices ASTROV's
map on the table. She unrolls it carefully. She closes her eyes
as she moves her finger-tips caressingly over the surface of the
map. She opens her eyes slowly. She looks at the door of VANYA's
study. She goes to the door.*)
Ivan. Ivan Petrovich. I'll be leaving soon. Won't you say
goodbye to me? Please. We've been friends for a long
time. I don't want to leave like this. (*No response.*) I know
how you feel. Please believe me. If only there was
something I could do!
(*ASTROV enters quickly through the hall door. He is wearing
a long, dark fur coat.*)

ASTROV: My god, but it's freezing out there. (*Puts his
doctor's bag on the dresser and goes into the dining room.*)
I need some brandy! I'll fill my flask for the journey!
(*YELENA looks down at her hands. She appears to be
strangely shy and uneasy. She lifts her head and parts her
lips as if to speak, but thinks better of it.
Short silence.*)

YELENA: And how is Telegin's wife?

ASTROV: (*Calling from the dining room.*) She gave him a
terrible fright. (*Enters while he is screwing the cap on a*

silver hip-flask.) Tearing off strips of wallpaper and shrieking like an owl. I'm afraid she might have to be committed one of these days... I told Telegin as much. The poor man started weeping when she spat out her false teeth and they broke into a thousand pieces. (*Looking at YELENA.*) I see you're ready.

YELENA: Yes. Everything's packed.

ASTROV: And how are you feeling?

YELENA: A bit nervous, of course. It's all been so sudden. And then, I've never been to the South. I don't really know what to expect. Won't you tell me something about it? Until last night I never knew you spent your childhood there. Strange how little I know about you. You really are a very mysterious man.

ASTROV: Odessa... In the summer there was a sweet sea-breeze. It used to blow in from the side of the Big Fountain lighthouse... Over the melon fields... (*Little laugh.*) But this was all so long ago. Everything's probably changed.

YELENA: And there was something else you said... About wanting to see the South again...

ASTROV: Just look at that! (*Holds out his one hand.*)

YELENA: (*Getting up quickly and moving to him.*) What is it?

ASTROV: The old bitch scratched me.

YELENA: (*Looking closely.*) How horrible. And so deep.

ASTROV: (*Going to his bag.*) I didn't even notice. Odd. (*Opens his bag.*) It must be the cold. Well, at least she didn't bite me. Did you know that a human bite is the most dangerous of all.

YELENA: No I didn't.

ASTROV: It can become septic faster than the bite of any other animal. (*Dabs iodine onto his hand. Gives a moan and closes his eyes.*)

YELENA: Let me... (*She takes his hand and blows on it.*)

ASTROV: There. It doesn't burn any more. (*Laughs.*) You're an angel of mercy Yelena Andreyevna.

YELENA: (*Little laugh. Moves away.*) That's what my mother used to do. Tell me Astrov, what did you mean when you said you might be going to the South?

ASTROV: (*Looking into his bag.*) That's odd.

YELENA: What is it?

ASTROV: I seem to be missing some morphine. Yes. I'm quite sure.

YELENA: But who could have taken it?

ASTROV: It happened before, do you remember?

YELENA: No. I can't say I do.

ASTROV: Before you left the last time.

YELENA: After that terrible scene when Vanya tried to shoot my husband?

ASTROV: Yes. After. Anyway, Sonya and I pleaded with him and he gave the morphine back.

YELENA: Yes... I think I do remember something.

ASTROV: Have you seen him this afternoon?

YELENA: No. He's been in there all day. With the door locked...

ASTROV: (*Going to the door.*) Ivan! Ivan Petrovich! You have something of mine and I want it back. (*Listens.*)

YELENA: (*Whispering.*) Do you hear anything?
(*ASTROV shakes his head.*)

YELENA: Good God... You don't think... Oh, that would be too horrible.

ASTROV: (*Speaking softly.*) Don't upset yourself. He's too cowardly for that. He'll just go on living his senseless life.

SONYA: (*Entering.*) Then you're back Mikhail. And how is Telegin's poor wife?

ASTROV: Won't you please try and talk to your uncle?

YELENA: He won't open the door.

SONYA: He's drinking. I'd rather not talk to him when he's been drinking. (*To YELENA.*) I managed to keep the biscuits down after all.

ASTROV: I don't want to alarm you...but he's stolen some of my morphine.

SONYA: Like last time?

ASTROV: Yes.

SONYA: And have you asked him to give it back?

YELENA: He won't talk to us.

SONYA: Oh, poor uncle... (*To YELENA.*) You've made him so wretched!

ASTROV: There's no time for that now. Get him to open the door.

SONYA: (*Going to the door.*) Uncle! Uncle! Dearest uncle, please answer me!
(*Silence.*)
You're frightening me! And you know I shouldn't be upset!

YELENA: We should try and break down the door.

ASTROV: (*To SONYA.*) Keep talking to him. He'll answer in a moment.

SONYA: Uncle Vanya! Uncle! Uncle! Oh Mother of God he's not answering. (*To YELENA.*) And all because of you. The first time I saw you here in this very room, I got goosebumps all over.

ASTROV: (*At the door.*) For god's sake Vanya, don't be a fool. You're distressing Sonya! You'll make her ill!

SONYA: (*Hysterical. Pounding on the door.*) Uncle, uncle, please... I can't bear it... I simply can't bear it!!

VANYA: (*Wrenches open the door. He is very drunk. He is unsteady on his feet and slurs his words. He is wearing the same dressing gown and slippers as in Act One.*) Why can't you leave me in peace?

SONYA: Uncle! God be praised!

ASTROV: Ivan, you have something of mine and I want it back.

SONYA: Uncle...you're terribly drunk. Terribly. Oh... I suddenly feel so dizzy.

VANYA: Yes, I'm drunk. I won't be sober again 'till I'm dead.

ASTROV: (*Taking SONYA's arm.*) Come and sit down. You've had a shock.

SONYA: (*Sitting.*) I feel awful.

ASTROV: Put your head between your knees. (*To VANYA.*) You took morphine out of my bag.

VANYA: What if I did?

ASTROV: Be reasonable Ivan Petrovich.

VANYA: What do you want me to do? Live this dreary life to please you? To hell with it!

NANNY: (*Off. Rather desperately.*) Sonya! Sonya.

ASTROV: Don't get up. I'll go. (*Quickly out.*)

VANYA: I'm tired of it all. I'm disgusted... Yes... Yes...
I disgust myself.

SONYA: How can you say that uncle?

VANYA: (*Makes a fist and starts beating himself on the chest.*)
Fool...fool...fool...

SONYA: Stop it uncle!

VANYA: (*To YELENA.*) All dressed up and ready to go.
Well, why not? (*He sways.*) Now that you have
your...royalties. (*Laughs.*) Is that what you call them?
Now you can escape... Leave this dreary life behind.
(*Takes a slim volume out of his dressing-gown pocket. Squints
at it.*)
'The Demise of Art, Posthumous essays by Professor A
Serebryakov.' My God, what a joke!

SONYA: How can you say that? My father always wanted
his work to be published. That's what he lived for.

VANYA: Well... It's a bit late isn't it? A bit late for the Herr
Professor?

SONYA: I can't bear it uncle.

ASTROV: (*Entering.*) What's wrong?

SONYA: He's insulting the memory of my father.

VANYA: Your father was a fool!

ASTROV: Come now Ivan Petrovich.

VANYA: You thought so too. You told me so. A fool! (*Points
at YELENA.*) He married that blood-sucking leech, didn't
he? Look at her...even now she's picking the bones of
her dead husband!

YELENA: How dare you speak to me like that! I had
nothing to do with the book! (*Coughs.*)

SONYA: She's right. It was me. I was going through father's
papers... I thought I owed it to him.

VANYA: Owed! What did he ever do for you?

SONYA: I also thought that if I could get something
published, we might get some money. What's wrong with
that? Heaven knows we need it. I didn't say anything
uncle, because I know you've always been jealous of my
father. But then they sent the money to her. (*Indicates
YELENA.*) And she hasn't given us a penny!

(*SONYA gives a stifled sob and runs from the room.*)

VANYA: (*Calling after her.*) Jealous of that old cuttlefish!
I could have been a poet! A philosopher! Anything
I wanted to be!

ASTROV: (*To VANYA.*) You're very drunk, Ivan Petrovich.
You should go and lie down. But for God's sake, give me
the morphine first.

VANYA: (*Moves towards the study door.*) Oh, to hell with you!
To hell with all of you! (*Turns. To YELENA.*) S'pose I'm
not clever enough for you. Why don't you go and marry
another Herr Professor. Go on! Another pos-thu-mous,
dried up ole stick. (*Turns and goes into the study.*)

ASTROV: (*Following him.*) Ivan, I want that morphine.

VANYA: (*Off.*) Here! (*Appears in the doorway.*) Here's your
precious morphine! (*Throws it into the room. It rolls onto
the carpet. VANYA shuts the door with a bang. From behind
the door.*) My name isn't Ivan! It's Jean!

ASTROV: His late mother used to call him that, do you
remember? (*He looks at his pocket-watch.*)
(*Short silence.*)

YELENA: (*Turning her face away.*) Don't look at me. My
nose goes red when I try not to cry. Oh, I wish I could
give back every rouble you've spent on me! But as it is,
I only have enough money to stay in a second-rate
boarding-house for a few months. I don't even care. As
long as I can get away. Get away from here. I don't even
care what happens to me.

ASTROV: I can understand that. My god.
(*Short silence.*)

YELENA: I'm still wondering about what you said
yesterday evening...

ASTROV: What do you mean?

YELENA: About...going to the South?

ASTROV: Oh. That. (*Short silence.*) Well...I might as well
tell you...I'm seriously thinking of getting on the train
with you tonight. Of going away and never coming back.
But I don't know if I'll have the nerve.

YELENA: I never thought...I never imagined...

ASTROV: Oh, don't worry. I'm not foisting myself on you. (*Short silence.*) A dissipated, second-rate country doctor. I know what you think of me.

YELENA: Please don't talk like that. Please. (*Turns away.*) I've got to know you – and respect you. The good work that you're doing. You're dedicated. What if I told you that...I've started caring for you. (*Little laugh.*) Quite desperately. What...would you say then?

ASTROV: (*Laugh.*) I'd know you were lying. Which is just as well, because I don't feel a passion for you any more. These last months...living so...intimately together...I don't know. It simply seemed to fade away. Maybe I was right. I used to believe that passionate love was a form of insanity. And when you come to your senses...you simply can't imagine what all the fuss was about. (*Laughs.*)

YELENA: Of course, you're quite right.

ASTROV: And I thought you were a romantic. (*Laughs.*)

YELENA: You taught me to be a realist, remember?

ASTROV: Oh yes. That's true. (*Moves about restlessly.*) No... I don't want to leave for any particular reason...Maybe it was you, talking about going South to the Black Sea... I don't know...But a few mornings ago I woke up and I suddenly realised that my life here is a complete sham. No, don't say anything. It's a fact. Oh! I've been trying to find some meaning...(*Opens the map on the table.*) Devoting myself to conserving forests...To curing cholera... (*He suddenly tears up the map.*)

YELENA: No!

ASTROV: Don't tell me you admire my maps after all. (*Laughs.*) No...The fact is that I can't really care about anything...or anyone. And I don't even know why. (*Short silence.*)

YELENA: What about your child?

ASTROV: Yes...I suppose that's the worst of all. I could only think of it as another wretch who should never have been born. No...I'll be the bastard who deserted his wife and his child. At least that will be the truth. But I have a conscience after all. And they'd be somehow so hopeless without me. It's been giving me sleepless nights. But if I don't go now I never will.

(*Short silence.*)

YELENA: If we leave at the same time...You know what they'll think.

(*Short silence.*)

ASTROV: Does it really matter to you?

(*YELENA looks at ASTROV. Short silence.*)

YELENA: No.

ASTROV: We understand each other, don't we?

YELENA: I suppose we do.

ASTROV: Well then... I don't see any reason why we couldn't keep each other company in Odessa. At least until we find something better to do.

(*Short silence.*)

Do you?

YELENA: No. I suppose not. (*Quiet and bitter.*) Until...we find something better to do.

ASTROV: Well, for now I won't think about it any more. I must go and ask Yakov if the sleigh is ready. We should be leaving. (*Exits rapidly.*)

(*Silence. YELENA sits very still, staring out in front of her. SONYA appears in the door. She seems strange, almost dazed.*)

SONYA: Nanna Marina soiled her sheets. I had to clean her. It was horrible... Horrible... I've scrubbed my hands. I...wanted to scrub off the skin.

YELENA: You'll have to do something about her. She must have family somewhere.

SONYA: She has no-one.

(*Short silence.*)

YELENA: Well, I'd better get ready. (*Gets up and picks up her fur hat from the small table.*) We'll have to take a bearskin for the sleigh. (*She opens the curtains and looks at herself in the dark window. She pins up a few strands of hair.*)

SONYA: (*Moving into the room.*) Nanny told me something. I don't quite understand it.

YELENA: (*Still looking at herself in the window, putting on her hat.*) It's still snowing. What did she tell you?

SONYA: She said Astrov came to see her this afternoon. He spoke to her for quite a while. He hardly ever does that now.

YELENA: I don't see anything strange about that.

SONYA: She said he took her face in his hands, and he told her that he's always had a great fondness for her. Then he kissed her on her forehead. She was so moved. She said he'd never done anything like that. She said he'd only done it once before. And after that he stayed away for more than a year. That was before we were married. She asked me if he was going very far away. And I said 'no, no...he's only going to be away for the night. Only going to stay over in town. He often does it. When he has a serious case'. But she wouldn't believe me. I told her...but she wouldn't believe me.

YELENA: Old people have strange ideas. (*Turning to her.*) So, what do I look like? Oh, what's wrong? Come now... Don't be sad.

(*The sound of sleigh bells. The garish flickering of sleigh torches can be seen through the window.*)

There's Yakov with the sleigh now. He's already lit the torches. Maybe in the summer you can all come and visit me. In Odessa or Yalta or wherever I'll be.

SONYA: Yes...maybe.

YELENA: (*Putting on her gloves.*) And then I'll be able to see your beautiful baby.

SONYA: I've never, ever seen the sea.

YELENA: Well, you must.

SONYA: (*Rubs her palm across her forehead.*) It's hard to imagine...something so endless.

(*Short silence.*)

YELENA: Sonya my dear... I wish we'd been kinder to each other... Oh, not just you and I... I mean all of us. We've been so... Oh... it's too hard to explain.

ASTROV: (*Entering. He is also wearing a fur hat.*) The sleigh's ready.

YELENA: Sonya was just saying that she can't imagine anything as vast as the sea.

SONYA: As...endless.

ASTROV: It's not just vast... No... It's also wild and restless.

(*Short silence.*)

We have to take the luggage now.

YELENA: Let me check everything again. Just to make sure. (*Exits.*)

(*Short silence.*)

ASTROV: It's not snowing too heavily. But there's a bitterly cold wind.

SONYA: Will you be home in the morning?

ASTROV: Probably late afternoon. There are some patients I must see.

SONYA: If you get back after dark, you'll be so cold. And so tired. I won't try to save wood. I'll make a big fire in the stove. (*Goes to him and touches his face.*) Oh, Mikhail... I'm so sorry.

ASTROV: What about?

SONYA: I've not been a good wife to you.

ASTROV: What nonsense.

SONYA: It's true. Always nagging. Being difficult. You see... I've been unhappy because I... expected too much from you. But I won't do that any more. I won't. You'll see...everything will be better from now on. Mikhail... Mikhail... You mean everything to me. (*Throws her arms around his neck and presses her head against his chest.*)

ASTROV: Ssh... Come now... Come now. (*He strokes her hair.*) You're being a silly girl. (*Gently unwinding her arms from around his neck.*) Don't talk like that. You're good and kind. And that's all that matters.

SONYA: (*Looking at him.*) And I haven't made you too unhappy?

ASTROV: My dearest Sonya...

YELENA: (*Entering.*) I'm so sorry to disturb you, but I can't find my small valise with the silver clasp. (*Going into the dining room.*) The house is so dark that I can hardly see a thing. (*Coming out again.*) I might have brought it in here... (*Looking about.*) But I can't imagine why I would have done that. (*Finding it behind the sofa.*) Here it is. How silly of me. Well... I suppose it's time to say goodbye. (*Goes to SONYA.*) Don't come out into the

hallway. It's warmer in here. (*Kisses her on both cheeks.*)
Look after yourself Sonya dear. (*Turns and exits quickly.*)
(*Short silence.*)

SONYA: Have you remembered...the bearskin for the
sleigh?

ASTROV: Yes. Yes, I have. Dearest Sonya...

SONYA: (*Noticing the torn map.*) Your map! Just look at it.

ASTROV: It doesn't matter.

SONYA: Who did that? Who tore it up?

ASTROV: I did, if you must know.

SONYA: But why? You've worked so hard. Why did you
do it?

ASTROV: It really doesn't matter.

SONYA: (*Frightened.*) But why did you do it? Why? Why?
You must tell me.

ASTROV: (*Angrily.*) Why can't you just leave it alone?
(*Short silence.*)
(*Goes to SONYA.*) Dearest Sonya... (*He takes her face in his
hands.*) There's one thing I always want you to remember.

SONYA: (*Whispering.*) And what is that?

ASTROV: Whatever happens, I always want you to know
that I have a really deep affection for you. A really deep
affection. (*He kisses her on her forehead.*) And now I have
to go.
(*SONYA looks completely stricken. ASTROV goes to the dresser
and picks up his doctor's bag.*)
Don't see me off. You must keep warm. Goodbye, my
dear. (*Exits rapidly.*)
(*SONYA stands completely motionless. Her face registers
profound shock. The sound of the heavy front-door closing.
After a while the sound of sleigh bells as the sleigh leaves.
SONYA moves slowly to a chair and sits down heavily. Slowly
the light from the torches becomes dim and then disappears.
She stares out in front of her. She seems totally dejected.*)

NANNY: Sonya!
(*Short silence.*)
Sonya!
(*SONYA gets up slowly and heavily and exits. The stage is
empty and there is complete silence. After a few moments, the*

front door opens and closes softly. Slow footsteps can be heard. ASTROV appears in the hall door. There are snowflakes on his hat and on his coat. He looks completely defeated. After a few seconds SONYA re-enters and looks up at the lamp. Slowly she becomes aware of ASTROV's presence.)

ASTROV: *(After a silence. Still standing in the doorway. Quietly.)* I decided I wouldn't go along to the station after all. I suddenly didn't feel very well.

SONYA: I think...you've been working too hard.

ASTROV: Yes. That must be it.

(Short silence. SONYA gets heavily onto the chair and turns down the lamp.)

SONYA: Then you can help me with Nanna Marina. She soiled her sheets. I did what I could, but I can't wash her alone.

ASTROV: Poor old woman. She'd be better off dead.

SONYA: *(Extending an arm.)* Won't you help me down?

(ASTROV moves to her and helps her down.)

I'm becoming so heavy. You're still wearing your hat.

ASTROV: Yes.

SONYA: *(Moving towards the door.)* It's wet. Remember to take it off in the hall.

(SONYA exits. ASTROV sits on the edge of a chair. He stares at the floor for a moment, then – with a violent gesture – he knocks his hat off his head.)

(Off.) Are you coming?

(ASTROV sits for another moment. Then he gets up, dutifully picks up his hat and exits to the hall. Short silence. VANYA opens the study door and puts his head around the door.)

VANYA: They're gone... They're gone. I thought it was very quiet. *(Comes further into the room. He is wearing a bright, crochet blanket around his shoulders.)* Sonya, where are you? Sonya! Sonya! *(Calling loudly in the direction of the hall.)* Sonya come and talk to me! Come and talk to me! Come and tell me those things you always tell me when I'm unhappy. Please. Sonya! *(Talking to himself.)* I'm cold... Cold... Always cold. Sonya! Sonya, please. I want to hear them now!

(A moment's silence.)

No-one. No one. I must go to sleep. Sleep...and dream the happy life of Ivan Petrovich. (*Sadly mocking. Mimicking SONYA.*) 'Poor uncle Vanya. We've known no happiness in our lives.' (*Shadows of the falling snow flutter across the walls.*) 'But wait, dear uncle. Wait. One day we shall have rest, you and I. Rest'.

(*A knock on the hall door.*)

Who's there?

(*TELEGIN appears in the door. He is wearing a rabbit-skin fur hat and a rabbit coat. He is holding a lantern.*)

Telegin? Is that you?

TELEGIN: It's me, Ivan Petrovich.

VANYA: My good old friend! Come in. Come in.

(*A loud bang.*)

Good God, what was that?

TELEGIN: It's the front door, Ivan Petrovich.

VANYA: Sounded like a shot.

TELEGIN: I'm sorry, I forgot to close it.

VANYA: For god's sake, come in and sit down! Why are you hovering like that?

TELEGIN: Yes Ivan Petrovich... (*Sits down at the table. He puts down the lamp in front of him.*) Can't stay very long. I'm sorry I was too late. I never said goodbye to Yelena Andreyevna.

VANYA: What a pity. You could have said (*He pronounces 'goodbye' comically – like a howl.*) 'Gooodbyeeeee Yelena Andreyevna. Gooodbyeee. (*Short laugh.*)

TELEGIN: Yes. I was late because I couldn't find my hat. (*Smiles. Touches his hat.*) But then I found it.

VANYA: Well, you'll never see her again. Never again! Never...

TELEGIN: Excuse me, Ivan Petrovich, but you can't say that. Just look at my wife. Coming back after all these years. I never gave up hope you see. And I never thought unkindly of her. How could I blame her. I'm such a miserable specimen of a man... But this evening she gave me quite a fright. Then doctor Astrov came and gave her an injection and she went straight to sleep. She's sleeping so peacefully now. I covered her up very

warmly before I left. But she always sleeps quietly next
to me. Quietly as a child. And she breathes so softly,
I can hardly hear her. But when she wakes up she
always wakes up at once. And opens her eyes wide.
Like this. (*Opens his eyes wide.*)
(*VANYA's head has dropped forward. He is snoring softly.*)
Yesterday morning when I saw the first snow, I woke
her up and I took her over to the window. (*As if reliving
the experience.*) 'Look, little dove. Just look. The snow
has filled up the hollows. Covered the trees. Like a
flood... A flood...with all the anger and the rushing
taken out of it.'
(*TELEGIN smiles tenderly. His smile becomes almost beatific
as the lights fade slowly to black.*)

The End.

ON THE LAKE
a tragi-comic dream play

to my daughter, Nina, who knows how to fly

Anything can happen; everything is possible and probable. On a slight groundwork of reality, imagination spins and weaves new patterns made up of memories, experiences, absurdities and improvisations. But a single consciousness holds sway over them all – that of the dreamer.

August Strindberg, preface to *A Dream Play*

'There's a theatre for you! Just the curtain and the two wings and beyond it – open space. No scenery. An open view of the lake and the horizon. We'll raise the curtain when the moon comes up.'

Kostia, Chekov's *The Seagull*

Characters

NINA
mid-twenties. Delicate and whimsical.
An actress in a provincial company

MOTHER (of NINA)
between thirty and forty. Wide-eyed and
highly-strung. Drowned herself in the lake
many years before

POLINA
between fifty and sixty. A brooding, big-boned
woman who is hard of hearing. In Arkadina's service

MASHA
thirty. Moody and erratic. Polina's daughter. She has a
toothache and her cheek is swollen

ARKADINA
between forty-five and fifty. A histrionic, ageing
actress who is mortally ill

On the Lake was first performed at the Rhodes Theatre Complex in Grahamstown, South Africa on 28 June 2001, as part of the Official Programme of the National Arts Festival, presented by the National Arts Festival and The First Physical Arts Theatre Company, with the following cast:

NINA, Brink Scholtz

MOTHER, Lucy Wylde

POLINA, Grethe Fox

MASHA, Anna Karien Otto

ARKADINA, Annelisa Weiland

Director, Reza de Wet

Setting

The action takes place in a room on the first floor of a decaying country house on a lake. The room is dusty and shadowy. The wallpaper is stained with damp and, in places, peeling off the walls. The door frames and doors are heavily and ornately carved. In Scenes 1 and 6 the furniture is covered with dust sheets. Back right is the hall entrance. Front left is the entrance to the bedroom. There is a window in the fourth wall, right. The large window, edged with patterns of stained glass, is entirely suggested by use of light. There is an ottoman right centre and a card table left, slightly to front. There is a small stool to the left of the table and an intricately patterned wicker chair to the right of it. An identical wicker chair is near the window, right front.

Music

The original music, created for the end of the play, is an integral part of the text.

Sound effects

Sound effects are extremely important and must be used only as described in the text. Some of the sound effects can be slightly over-emphasised to underscore the dream-like quality of the play.

Pantomimes

There are five pantomimes which form a link between the scenes. The pantomimes enhance the rhythmic, musical quality of the text while also reinforcing the 'dream' aspect of the play.

Style

The sombre quality of the play should be carefully balanced by the comic and, at times, even grotesquely comic elements. The action of the play should be buoyant and not weighed down by meaningful subtext.

Time

Summer 1910

Prologue

The lights are faded up slowly. The stage is almost in black except for bright moonlight falling through the window. A small valise has been left on the ottoman. After a short while, sounds can be heard of someone moving about on the floor below. The shutters are opened. A door slams. Then, after a few moments, footsteps can be heard getting closer. A glimmer of light can be seen through the hall doorway as NINA slowly and wearily mounts the stairs. She appears in the doorway carrying a lamp. She looks dishevelled and utterly exhausted. She is wearing a loose coat and a shawl over her head. She picks up the valise and moves towards the bedroom door. For a moment she pauses uncertainly in the doorway and then exits to the bedroom. After a few seconds she re-appears. She stands in the doorway looking at the moonlit window. She has taken off her coat and her shawl ans has left the lamp in the bedroom. A soft glimmer can be seen through the bedroom door. Slowly, as if mesmerised, she moves towards the window and stands looking out. She seems wistful and deeply sad. She gives a little cry and presses her hand to her mouth. She continues to look out. Slowly her intense waringess overcomes her and she sinks down in the chair near the window. Gently her head falls back and her eyes close...

Scene 1

Gusts of wind can be heard throughout the scene. It is dawn and a pale, bluish light falls through the window. Much of the stage can only be dimly seen. NINA is still sitting on the chair near the window. Nina's MOTHER is standing in the right, back corner looking at her. She is wearing a white nightdress and is very pale.

MOTHER: Why did you open the shutters? You're letting the light in. (*Touches her eyelids with the tips of her fingers.*) It hurts...my eyes.

NINA: I know you're...looking at me. (*Short silence.*) The moment I came into this house...I knew you were still here, Mother. Shadowing me. Still. After all these years. I thought...after Father died...you'd disappear. But here you are. I can remember what it feels like...when you're

near. It used to frighten me when I was small... Sensing
you in the long passages...and on the dark stairs.
(*Fearful.*) I was afraid you would suddenly...come
closer...and touch me. (*Shuddering.*) And I thought how
cold it would be. Your touch. (*Short silence.*)
(*MOTHER gives a long sigh.*)
And every night...I dreamt about you.

MOTHER: (*Moving a little towards her.*) I wish I...could
dream. Wish I could...sleep.

NINA: Don't come any closer, Mother. Keep...away. I can
feel you now...creeping towards me. Like a
coldness...seeping into me. Dreadful.

MOTHER: Oh...I just wanted to come...a little closer. I've
been so sad...and lonely. (*Tearful.*) So...lonely. Why must
you be so...unkind?
(*NINA turns her head away.*)
Oh...I can see you still blame me. After all...it happened
so many years ago. And surely, there are worse things
than drowning oneself. Surely there are worse things
than that! (*Tearful. Short silence.*) And come away from
the window. You mustn't...look at the water. It's cold...
and black...and deep. (*A cry.*) And why, why did you
open the shutters? Close them! Close them! (*Short silence.*
Frightened. In a low voice.) I can see...the water moving.
Light reflecting patterns on the walls... Across the floor.
And there...in the glass of the open window. (*A cry.*) Why
do you keep looking?

NINA: I'm not looking at the water, Mother. I'm looking
across the lake at Madame Arkadina's estate.

MOTHER: That actress. She had a terrible reputation when
I was alive.
(*NINA gasps.*)

MOTHER: (*Frightened.*) What is it?

NINA: (*Almost to herself, looking out of the window.*) Someone
has lit a lamp upstairs. I can see the light glimmering
through the window. And...smoke rising from the
chimney. (*Slight intake of breath.*) Oh...everything is as it
used to be. I can hardly believe it. Even Kostia's little
stage is still there...near the edge of the water. (*Her head*

droops.) Only I have changed. I used to dream of being like her. A great actress. And what has become of me? I play bit-parts in a Provincial company.

MOTHER: Why don't you look at me? I'm still your mother. I...haven't changed. And talk to me. Why don't you talk to me? I so long...to have a conversation. Maybe...you're frightened. Perhaps...my voice sounds strange. It's just...that I'm not used to speaking. Years and years of being quiet. (*Tearful.*) What was the use of speaking if he couldn't hear me? I ask you?

(*NINA rests her head in her hands. A gust of wind. An awning flaps in the wind.*)

NINA: (*Startled.*) What was that?

MOTHER: The broken awning...flapping in the wind. After she died...he didn't care about anything. The house... went to ruin. (*Sighs.*) I used to take such pride in this house.

NINA: I thought it was a bird...with a broken wing. (*The awning flaps.*) What a sad sound. (*Looks out.*)

MOTHER: When the wind blows...there are waves on the lake. (*Scared.*) Are there waves on the lake now?

NINA: Small waves. (*The awning flaps. Short silence.*)

MOTHER: Talk to me. (*Short silence.*) Please talk to me. I only hear the wind...the cries of birds and the lapping...of the water. (*A cry.*) I'm so unhappy. Don't you care at all? After all...I'm still your mother!

NINA: Why should I care? What have you ever done for me? (*MOTHER whimpers.*) When you walked into the water, you only thought about yourself!

MOTHER: What do you know! You know nothing!

NINA: Isn't that how it was, Mother? Isn't it? (*MOTHER cries.*)

MOTHER: You don't know what I've suffered. You don't! Once...I stood at that...window... Looking out. And then...I saw *her*...in the garden. She was... wearing a white dress...and looking...up at me. That... hideous woman! Even...when I saw her...she kept looking...looking...cursing me! (*Little cry.*) I mustn't think of that. (*Shivers.*) It makes me feel...so cold...so cold. (*Wrings her hands.*) Don't let me think about...that. (*Whispering.*) It...frightens me so. My nerves are bad, you see. Very bad.

NINA: (*Wearily.*) It doesn't matter any more. I don't want to know. Oh, Mother, why don't you go away and leave me alone!

(*MOTHER whimpers.*)

NINA: Just...go away! (*Presses her hand over her eyes.*) I'm so tired. I travelled all night. So...far. I never slept on the train.

MOTHER: I don't know what you have to complain about. At least you travel... See other places. And just look at me. Trapped in this gloomy house. Year after year. But I suppose I can't expect any sympathy from you.

NINA: (*As if to herself. Looking out of the window.*) There is the room where I saw Kostia for the last time... A terrible wind in the trees. And thin...cold rain. Kostia said I should stay with him. That I would be warm and... safe. But I told him that I still loved Trigorin... Then I embraced him...and ran out into the night. (*Weeps quietly.*)

MOTHER: Turn around and talk to me!

NINA: (*Gets up.*) I should get some rest (*Moves towards the bedroom.*) I should try and sleep before the sun comes up.

MOTHER: Oh, please don't go! Please don't leave me! I haven't had company for such a long time.

(*NINA pauses at the bedroom entrance.*)

MOTHER: Please. I beg you. Stay! Talk to me!

NINA: I don't want to talk to you any more Mother. I just want to be quiet.

MOTHER: (*Desperately.*) Please...I'll tell you, if you want me to! I'll tell you what happened that night. You've always asked me! Maybe then...you'll understand.

(*Short silence. NINA turns and looks at her.*)

(*A cry.*) Oh...my heart is beating...so fast... (*Short silence.*)
That night...I woke up...and saw your father...standing
at the window. I thought *she* must be out there. Calling
him. So...I tip-toed...and I stood next to him. I looked
out but there...was no-one there. I...touched his
arm...and called his name...but he didn't look at me. I
started crying...bitterly...but... (*Little gasp.*) ...he closed
the shutters...and put out...the light. (*Wails softly.*)
Oh...oh...oh...I had...nowhere to go... Nowhere...to
go... There was only...the water. The cold...cold...
deep...black...water. (*Cries.*) Now...see what you've done.
You've gone and upset me!

NINA: (*Quietly.*) I know...how you felt, Mother. I know
it...too well. If only...I could tell you...

MOTHER: But even then...I couldn't leave him. I had to
come back...to be near him. At night they would sleep...
with their arms around each other... (*A cry.*)

NINA: All they wanted was to be alone together.
Father...started hating me. And she... (*Bitterly.*) my
'stepmother'...

MOTHER: And he called her his 'turtle dove'. (*Small cry.*)
I'll never understand what he saw in her. Never. And that
cheap scent. I used to smell it everywhere. It gave me
such a headache. (*Pause.*) When she died...I was alone
with him. Always very close to him. Once he stopped on
the stairs and said 'Who is there?' but when I spoke...he
didn't hear me. (*Pause.*) I was standing at the foot of his
bed the night he died. He opened his eyes very wide...
but he didn't see me. (*Gives a long sigh.*) After that...I
wanted to leave this place. I am so tired. I want to go
somewhere...very dark...and quiet. (*Little sigh of longing.*)

NINA: (*Gently.*) Why don't you, Mother?

MOTHER: How can I leave? Every door...leads out onto
the lake! And I don't want to see it. No! Not ever again!
(*Gives a stifled sob.*) I...don't want to see it.

NINA: For me...it's just the same. I can't leave either. Oh,
I've tried. The company is hardly in a town for more
than a night. Every morning, I get on the train. Every
evening...my destination is the same. (*Moves to the*

window.) As soon as I sleep...I drift back there. That old house... (*Looks out of the window.*) The garden... The lake...It looks just the same. There's *her* room. The shutters are open. So...she's here... Everything...just the same. And so much closer than I remember. I feel as if I can stretch out my hand...and touch...the walls...the windows...the tall cypress tress.

(*MOTHER gives a long, tearful sigh, as the lights fade to black and the music is brought up.*)

Pantomime

The lights and sound for the pantomime are very specific and remain the same for all pantomimes. During the pantomime, the lights are very low. Wave patterns wash over the floor, the furniture and the walls. During the pantomimes NINA's movements are slow and dreamlike. The sound of the wind intensifies as the pantomime lights are brought up. NINA is still standing at the window. She blinks slowly and opens her eyes as if waking up. She looks about her. She seems confused, almost dazed. At first she moves a little uncertainly, as if exploring unfamiliar territory, then she crossses to the back of the ottoman. She lifts the seat and looks inside. She lifts out a billowing white dress, holds it up and looks at it. Sadly she puts it back. She takes out a large story book bound in green leather. She closes the ottoman. She holds the book close to her and looks around uncertainly. Then she moves to the table. She puts the book on the table and sits down on the stool. As she pages through the book, she yawns. Her head droops onto her arms. Her eyes close as the pantomime lights fade out. The wind can still be heard in the black.

Scene 2

The lights come up slowly. Late afternoon. Bright light falls through the window and, by contrast, the rest of the room seems shadowy. NINA is asleep at the table with her head on her arms. POLINA is standing near her, peering at her. She is wearing a black headscarf, a black dress, and a black shawl with long fringes. There is a basket over her arm. After a few moments, she leans over and touches NINA on the shoulder. NINA starts awake. She looks confused and frightened.

POLINA: Is it you, Nina Mikhailovna? Is it you? I thought... you were your mother. (*Puts her hand on her heart.*) Gave me quite a turn.

NINA: ...Polina?

POLINA: (*Continues to peer at her.*) You've grown so thin, Nina Mikhailovna! And quite sallow. (*Shakes her head and clicks her tongue. Gesture.*) As if...your mother had risen from the grave.

NINA: (*Half asleep, still confused.*) Polina...is it?

POLINA: I'm sure you hardly recognise me. You see a broken woman before you, Nina Mikhailovna. (*Sighs.*) All these years...I've been nothing but a slave. Worked my fingers to the bone. (*Sighs.*) And for what, I ask you? (*Continues to peer at NINA.*) Your eyes are very big, Nina Mikhailovna. I seem to remember that they were smaller. (*Shakes her head.*) But I must be wrong. My memory...is failing me. Just look at this table! Dear, oh dear, oh dear. We wondered if you were coming back. So many rumours flying about. Someone said that you'd died recently. This floor hasn't been polished in years! Another person said they'd seen you in town. Look at this dust! And your mother was so proud of this house. And then...we also heard that you'd already been and gone. But here you are, Nina Mikhailovna, here you are.

NINA: Yes. I can hardly believe it. (*Rubs her eyes. Short silence.*) I've been looking...at my old story book. Wonderful...strange pictures of witches and innocent young girls.

POLINA: You'll have to speak up, Nina Mikhailovna. On top it all I've gone rather deaf. I hope you don't mind if I sit down Nina Mikhailovna. My feet are really killing me.

NINA: Please do. (*Stifles a yawn.*)

POLINA: (*Pulls out a chair. Sighs.*) No...no...I'm not what I used to be. (*Puts the basket on the table and sits down heavily.*) I've brought you some apples from our orchard.

NINA: Thank you. I still remember them. (*Picks up an apple. Loudly.*) The...sweetest apples in the world!

POLINA: Be careful of worms! They're not as nice as they used to be! (*Short silence.*) Everybody thought that you'd come back when your father died. But after the way he treated you, I wasn't really surprised. (*Leans forward.*) I went to see him when they laid him out. So pale and shrivelled and dressed in a moth-eaten suit. (*Sighs.*) It's been a black year. The cholera also took my husband and Madame Arkadina's poor brother.

NINA: I'm sorry. I didn't know.

POLINA: You're an actress. We're just unimportant people. Why should you know anything about us?

NINA: And...how is Masha?

POLINA: (*Sighs.*) My poor Masha. She'll be here soon. She stopped off to throw some crumbs on Kostia's grave. To make the sparrows come she says. Because then he's not so lonely! (*Sighs.*) She's got queer fancies that girl. Ever since Kostia died. (*Darkly.*) Of course, he's not buried on hallowed ground.

NINA: Poor Madame Arkadina. What a terrible thing. I can still hardly believe it.

POLINA: And you didn't come to Kostia's funeral either. I must say, I was very surprised. He used to be so fond of you. So fond of you.

NINA: I didn't know when he died. We were touring, you see! Never more than a day in the same place! (*As if to herself.*) But somehow...I must have had a feeling... because for months I've been having such...sad and tender dreams about him.

POLINA: Speak up!

NINA: (*Loudly.*) As soon as I hear I came back! When we were close to Yellietz, I got on the train and travelled all night to get here! (*To herself.*) The wheels on the track kept saying his name: Kos-tia, Kos-tia, Kos-tia.

POLINA: (*Darkly.*) Well, I'm sorry you were too late. (*Pause.*) Now where was I? Ah yes...poor Masha. How long has it been now since Kostia shot himself? Seven...eight months? She still goes to the cemetery every day. Prays for his soul every night. (*Sighs.*) And when he was alive...he ran after another woman...but

you know that better than anyone Nina Mikhailovna...
(*Shakes her head.*) Just...throwing her life away! She'll end
up with nothing...like me! (*Extremely agitated.*) You can't
throw your life away for a man who doesn't appreciate
you! (*Beats her breast.*) I know, Nina Mikhailovna!
Believe me! I know!

MASHA: (*Calling off.*) Where are you?

POLINA: (*Groans as she gets up. Goes to the window and leans
out.*) Up here! The door's open! (*Sighs. Returns to her seat.*)
She's still wearing her apron. As slovenly as ever.
(*Sound of the front door being opened and creaking on its
hinges. A sudden gust of wind enters the room. POLINA's
shawl flaps out behind her, NINA's hair is blown across her
face and the pages of the open book flutter like the frantic
beating of wings. Footsteps can be heard on the stairs and
MASHA's heavy panting.*)
(*Holding onto her shawl. Calls in the direction of the landing.*)
Close the door! Can't you ever close a door behind you!!
(*To NINA.*) If I've told her once, I've told her a thousand
times! God give me strength. What am I going to do
with that girl, Nina Mikhailovna? I'm all she's got in the
world! A child like that is such a burden to a mother.
(*Sound of receding footsteps and the heavy front door being
closed. The wind drops. Footsteps approaching. MASHA enters
from the landing. She is extremely out of breath. Her hair
looks dishevelled. She is wearing a shapeless black dress, a
floral apron and heavy shoes. Her shoelaces are untied.*)
You were right! Here she is.

NINA: Masha?

POLINA: (*To MASHA.*) She's very changed. Looks just like
her mother.

MASHA: I knew you'd come, I had a dream about it.

POLINA: Speak up my girl, you know I can't hear!

MASHA: I wasn't talking to you!

POLINA: Always muttering behind my back.

NINA: How have you been?

MASHA: (*Defiant.*) You won't know me, Nina Mikhailovna.
I'm quite a different person. Do you remember how sad
I used to be? I drank too much vodka and I always had

a headache. (*Tearful.*) I was such...a poor...miserable girl. It makes me unhappy...just to think of it.

(*Starts weeping quietly.*)

POLINA: (*Threatening.*) Stop that.

(*MASHA stops and puts her hand in front of her mouth.*)

(*To NINA, meaningfully.*) She's not been herself since Kostia died. (*To MASHA.*) And why haven't you tied your laces my girl?.

MASHA: I couldn't! I was in a hurry! (*To NINA.*) But now... everything is different. I'm always happy. I smile and hum all day. (*Trips over her shoelaces.*)

POLINA: Come and sit down.

MASHA: (*Sitting down.*) I knew you were coming. I had a dream. No-one believed me, Nina Mikhailovna. But I can see things.

POLINA: What did you say? Speak up!

MASHA: (*Loudly to POLINA.*) I said I can see things!

POLINA: That's the truth, Nina Mikhailovna, that's the truth. (*Smashes her fist down on the table.*) Cockroaches are filthy things. I saw three of them on the stairs. (*Sweeps the cockroach off the table.*) That's what happens when you leave house standing empty. (*Suddenly screams at MASHA.*) And you've left mud all over the floor! Can't you ever wipe your feet?

MASHA: (*Sulky.*) Oh, leave me alone! Just leave me alone!

POLINA: (*Outraged.*) Do you hear how she speaks to me? My own flesh and blood! Now where was I? Oh yes, she had two dreams. One on a Sunday and one on a Monday. Come now, tell Nina Mikhailovna about your first dream, my girl.

MASHA: No, please, I don't want to!

POLINA: Tell her!

MASHA: (*Unwillingly.*) The train...stopped. First...a tall man got out, wearing Kostia's dressing gown. And then you got out. The train left and you were all alone because the porter was sleeping and snoring. You came up to me and asked, 'do you know the way home?' I said, 'that way,' and you walked off very slowly. Then I woke up. (*Sullen.*) Because my mother was shaking me.

POLINA: (*To NINA.*) What was she saying about me?

NINA: She said she woke up because you were shaking her!

POLINA: (*Angrily.*) She'll sleep all day if I don't wake her!

MASHA: But you weren't in travelling clothes. (*Tearful.*) You were wearing your white dress. The one you wore in Kostia's play. (*Takes snuff.*)

POLINA: (*To NINA.*) She still has that filthy habit. (*Sighs.*)

NINA: (*Wistful.*) Oh yes...Kostia's play. My father and my stepmother locked me up...but I climbed down a tree and ran all the way to the estate. Kostia was so relieved to see me.

POLINA: I didn't hear that.

(*MASHA sneezes. Wipes her nose with a stained handkerchief.*)

NINA: (*Smiles sadly. Loudly to POLINA.*) I'm talking about the night I acted in Kostia's play!

POLINA: And would you believe it, Nina Mikhailovna, they're putting on that same play this very night!

NINA: Who's putting on a play?

(*MASHA stares at NINA. Her mouth is slightly open.*)

POLINA: Don't keep mentioning his name, Nina Mikhailovna, or you'll set poor Masha off again! (*Pause, wrings her hand.*) Why we're here, Nina Mikhailovna, is to...ask you what you are going to do with all this now that it's yours. Are you going to sell it...or keep it? Lopakhin will probably want to buy it, but I wouldn't trust him. I can tell you things about him...

NINA: (*Agitated.*) I don't know. I haven't really thought.

(*MASHA is staring at NINA. Her mouth is slightly open.*)

POLINA: Speak up.

NINA: I don't know!

POLINA: (*Suddenly very loud. To MASHA.*) Close your mouth, my girl, or you'll swallow a fly! And don't stare! It's rude!

MASHA: She's really here. It makes me feel...so funny. Maybe...if I dip a towel in cold water...and put it on my head...she'll disappear into thin air.

POLINA: She'll do no such thing. Please forgive her, Nina Mikhailovna. Now, where was I? Oh, yes. (*Smiling and rubbing her hands together.*) Better to keep the house for a time, that's what I think. Not to make up your mind right away. Don't you agree, Masha?

NINA: That may be for the best!

(*The distant sound of hammering as if nails are being knocked into wood. The sound continues until otherwise indicated in the text.*)

POLINA: In that case...Nina Mikhailovna...we want to offer you our services. Masha and I. Aren't you going to say anything, Masha?

MASHA: Yes. Offer our services.

POLINA: To stay here in the house when it's empty. There are vandals and thieves in these parts. They'll steal the windows out of the walls. What do you say?

NINA: Thank you very much, but I don't think that will be necessary!

POLINA: (*Suddenly very angry.*) Oh, so we're not good enough to stay in your house? To share it with cockroaches and rats!

NINA: That's not true! I just want everything to say the same...until I've decided what to do!

MASHA: A large house just standing empty! Very selfish of you, Nina Mikhailovna!

POLINA: Be quiet, Masha! (*Snorts.*) Well...I suppose we'd better be on our way then. Help me up, my girl.

(*MASHA helps her up. A low moan, tearful.*)

(*To MASHA.*) The truth is, my poor Masha, we have nowhere else to go. Soon we won't have a roof over our heads. (*Starts keening.*) What will become of us? What will become of us?

NINA: (*Loudly.*) Is Madame Arkadina...sending you away?

POLINA: No, it's not that. It won't be long now...

NINA: (*Loudly.*) But...is Madame Arkadina ill?

POLINA: (*Meaningful.*) Dying, Nina Mikhailovna.

MASHA/POLINA: (*Together.*) Dying!

NINA: (*Shocked and confused.*) But...I haven't heard anything.

POLINA: Tells everyone...she's resting in the country. If you don't believe me ask Masha. She helps to dress her every morning. (*To MASHA.*) Go on...tell her what she looks like under all that rouge.

MASHA: A terrible yellow colour. And a red scar growing... (*Draws a line up her torso.*) from here to here. And so thin...you can see the bones under the skin.

POLINA: You see. That's why Trigorin has been here all these months.

NINA: (*Shocked.*) Trigorin? Is he here? I didn't think he would be here.

POLINA: He's waiting to inherit the estate. To sell it to Lophakin, the land-developer. The two of them. Like vultures!

NINA: Dying. (*Shakes her head.*) It's like a bad dream. Poor Madame Arkadina. (*Loudly.*) The poor woman!

POLINA: Don't waste your pity. She cursed you often enough when you went off with... (*Sarcastic.*) her precious Trigorin! (*Claps her hand over her mouth.*) I'm sorry if I've spoken out of turn. As soon as she's gone, the house will be pulled down. (*Outraged.*) They want to put up a tea-garden and a pavilion for regattas.

NINA: (*Distressed.*) The...house? I love that house. (*Loudly.*) Such a nice house!

POLINA: You don't want to see it now. Death-watch beetles in the walls. Isn't that so, Masha?

MASHA: They gnaw so loudly, they keep me awake! (*Shuddering sigh.*)

POLINA: (*Sighs.*) Soon it will all gone.. My whole life I've slaved on that estate. Every night I dream that we wander around in the dark. Cold...and lost...and hungry. (*Tearful.*) Nowhere to go.
(*NINA goes to the window and looks out.*)
But what does it matter? Everything has to come to an end. (*Sighs. Very pathetic.*) Soon... I'll also be going to my grave.
(*MASHA crosses herself.*)

NINA: It's hard to believe. It all seems so...impossible.
(*MASHA takes snuff, sneezes loudly.*)
(*Looking out.*) And what did you say about the play? Are they putting on a play? (*Covering her ears. On the verge of hysteria.*) What is that hammering?

POLINA: (*To MASHA.*) What is she saying?

MASHA: She's asking if they're putting on a play.

POLINA: So they are, so they are. They're even repairing the old stage. What a waste.

NINA: (*Confused and distressed.*) Which play?

MASHA: The one you were in. (*Sullen.*) With your fancy dress...and your made-up face.

NINA: (*Extremely confused.*) But...I don't understand... (*Loudly to POLINA.*) Why are they putting on Kostia's play?

POLINA: I've asked you not to keep mentioning his name, Nina Mikhailovna! Think of my poor child!

NINA: (*Desperately.*) But why? She doesn't even like the play!

POLINA: Oh, Madame feels guilty, if you ask me. Spending all this money on her poor son's play. Getting people to come all the way from Moscow. (*With disgust.*) When he was alive, she didn't even look at him! (*Low voice.*) She wants to make things right before she goes, that's what I think. She's frightened of dying. (*Darkly.*) Of hellfire and damnation! (*Groans as she gets up.*)

MASHA: (*Quietly. Hissing.*) And you weren't even good in the play. That's what Madame Arkadina said.

POLINA: (*Moves towards NINA.*) Nina Mikhailovna, say you'll think about it. Don't just say no. What else will we do? (*Tearful.*) Where must we go? (*Sinks down on the ottoman.*)

NINA: (*Distressed.*) Yes. I'll...think about it!

POLINA: (*Grabs her hand and kisses it.*) Bless you! Bless you!

NINA: (*Draws her hand away.*) Please... (*Turns away from the window.*)

POLINA: (*Fawning.*) You're just as good and kind as your poor mother used to be.

(*The sound of hammering stops.*)

NINA: (*With disbelief.*) Are they...performing it tonight? I can hardly believe it. (*Sits on the ottoman.*)

MASHA: (*Hissing.*) Yes. An actress from Moscow will play your part. She looks like you. The way you used to look.

POLINA: What did you say?

MASHA: I'm saying that an actress from Moscow is playing the part!

POLINA: But her dress isn't as nice as yours. Very plain. (*Pause.*) I will come back tomorrow to hear what you've decided. I'll pray all night. (*Wails histrionically.*) 'Oh, dear God, let Nina Mikhailovna decide to have mercy on two poor, desperate women. Guide her and open her heart!'

MASHA: Amen.

POLINA: That's what I'll pray for. Come, on Masha. We have work to do.

MASHA: (*To NINA.*) Tonight...when the curtain opens and the moon rises, Nina Mikhailovna won't be acting. And (*Tearful.*) Kostia won't be watching. Only me. In my usual place. In the back row. (*Tearful and bitter.*) Sitting on a kitchen chair! And nobody will speak to me. They couldn't be bothered. Won't even notice that I'm there!

POLINA: Calm yourself my girl. (*To NINA.*) She is getting quite hysterical. Since Kostia died. She gets worked up over every little thing.

MASHA: But I won't let it worry me. I don't care about them any more. I'm not poor, sad Masha as I used to be. No. I'm happy. All day...I'm happy. (*Starts humming loudly.*)

POLINA: Come now. We have to go and make the stew. We cut vegetables all morning. That's why our hands smell so terribly of onions. We would look after the house. You can trust us. (*Puts the basket back on the table.*) Dust...scrub ...sweep in all the corners. Kill the cockroaches and the spiders and the rats! But before we go, you must tell Nina Mikhailovna your second dream, my girl. She must tell you Nina Mikhailovna.

MASHA: (*Pleading.*) No please, I don't want to!

NINA: Really, I'd rather not...

POLINA: Tell her!

MASHA: We were watching the play...the moon rose and then the curtain opened. You were on the stage, Nina Mikhailovna in your white dress. You were standing... looking at the water...you turned around slowly and then

...I saw that your face...that it was Kostia's face...and he ...looked the way he did just after he died. His eyes very wide...looking...but not seeing anything. His face...so white... And a round...black hole... (*Lifts her hand slowly and presses her finger against her forehead.*) in his forehead. (*She starts sobbing and runs from the room.*)
(*Nina gives a gasp.*)

POLINA She'll never get over it. Never! Poor Masha! My poor child. She lost her only chance of happiness when he died. And since then she's...well...she's not been quite right (*Taps her head.*) When they were small...they were always playing together...everyone said 'One day they'll be married and be happy for ever.' And they would have been. But then you came along with your wiles and your simpering. You took him away from her and you didn't even want him! In your heart Nina Mikhailovna, in your heart, you know that's true! Because of you...she has nothing! The least you can do...the very least...is to give us a place to stay!! A roof over our heads!! You owe us that much, as God is my witness!! You owe us!!!

MASHA: (*Appears in the doorway.*) I'm going to the graveyard. (*Weeps. Exits.*)

POLINA: Poor child...poor child...my poor child. (*Weeps.*)

Pantomime

The sound of the wind intensifies. When the pantomime lights are brought up NINA is still sitting on the ottoman. She blinks and opens her eyes as if she's just woken up. She rubs her face, then stretches slightly. She seems dazed and disorientated. She gets up and moves towards the bedroom entrance. At the entrance she hesitates, then turns and looks about uncertainly. She notices the book on the table. She moves towards the table and sits down on the wicker chair. She turns the book around and starts paging through it. She yawns. Her head droops and her eyes close. She falls asleep with her head in the crook of her arm. The pantomime lights fade out. The wind can still be heard in the black.

Scene 3

The lights fade up. Mid-afternoon. Indirect light falls through the window and the light in the room is diffused. The basket has been removed from the table. NINA is asleep on the chair, left centre. ARKADINA is standing in the hall entrance with POLINA next to her. She is dressed as before but now carries an ear-trumpet. ARKADINA is wearing a frilly mauve dress, a large hat with an elaborate spray of feathers and a veil covering her face. She is breathless.

ARKADINA: I...can't...breathe. (*Gasps.*) Can't...breathe.
　　(*NINA wakes up and sees ARKADINA and POLINA.*
　　POLINA takes ARKADINA's elbow and leads her to the
　　ottoman.)
　　I see...spots...in front of my eyes.
POLINA: Sit down.
　　(*ARKADINA sits.*)
ARKADINA: And there...is a faint and terrible ringing in
　　my ears.
　　(*POLINA tries to lift her legs onto the ottoman.*)
　　Take your hands off me! (*Gives a few rasping breaths.*)
　　Because...I'm not myself today...you think you can take
　　liberties? (*Gasps. Looks at POLINA. Points at the ear-trumpet.*)
　　Why aren't you using that? Heaven only knows, I paid
　　enough for it!
NINA: (*Getting up.*) How do you do, Madam?
　　(*POLINA starts and ARKADINA gives a little gasp.*)
POLINA: (*Reluctantly lifts the ear-trumpet to her ear. To*
　　NINA.) She...makes me use this thing. I'm ashamed.
　　It's...not natural.
ARKADINA: (*Gesture.*) Oh, shoesh! (*To NINA.*) I can't...
　　shout all the time. It would ruin my voice. (*To POLINA.*)
　　I've asked you not to...touch me so roughly.
POLINA: (*Almost as a threat.*) If you don't want me to help
　　you...maybe I should call Trigorin.
ARKADINA: (*With difficulty.*) You will...never...call
　　Trigorin! Whatever happens! Never! Do you...
　　understand me? He...hates...unpleasantness! (*Leaning*
　　back.) It's...this terrible heat. It...must be ninety in...the
　　shade. (*A grimace of pain. Turns her head and focuses on*

NINA for the first time.) Is it Nina? I wondered why we didn't hear from you.

NINA: (*Getting up.*) I'm so sorry, Madame...but I only found out a short while ago. I want to express my sincerest condolences.

ARKADINA: I'm not surprised you didn't know. I suppose your little company was touring in some remote part of the country. Of course... (*Falteringly.*) I was completely shattered. (*Bravely.*) But life has to go on. (*Peers at her.*) Come closer...and let me see you.
(*NINA approaches ARKADINA.*)
That's close enough... (*Looks at her.*) I...would hardly have known you. (*Short silence while she looks at her.*) Dear Nina...I hope you don't mind me saying so...but you seem...to have let yourself go. It really is...such a shame. (*Lifts the veil with a shaking hand.*) You were...such a lovely thing. The...precious bloom of youth...has to be...preserved...so carefully. Until...just a...few years ago...men treated me...as tenderly...as if I were...a young girl. But...of course...at the moment...I look...quite ghastly. (*Opening her handbag.*) I've...been ill, you see. (*Rummages in the handbag.*) It isn't easy...believe me. Every minute...of the day...you have to fight... against the ravages of time. Women...don't have that kind of...dedication any more. (*To POLINA.*) Where...is my little mirror? I...didn't bring my little mirror. You should have...reminded me!

POLINA: You must look after your own things! (*To NINA.*) You must have been asleep, Nina Mikhailovna. Your cheek is all creased.

ARKADINA: (*To NINA.*) I...need to take off my hat. To...freshen up a little. Do you...have a boudoir?

NINA: There is a mirror in the bedroom. (*Indicates the entrance to the bedroom left front.*)

ARKADINA: Thank you. (*Tries to get up, but cannot. To POLINA. Pathetic.*) Help me!
(*POLINA helps her.*)
Don't pull!
(*POLINA supports her as she walks to the door.*)

(*Going towards the door to NINA.*) The thing is...I've lost
so much weight. And it always...shows up in one's face.
Don't push!
(*ARKADINA and POLINA exit.*)
(*From the bedroom.*) I suppose it's the life...she's been
leading. Dragging herself around the country...in that
second-rate little company.

POLINA: Be quiet. She'll hear you.

ARKADINA: (*As before.*) She was very ambitious.
Disappointment is so bad...for the complexion. And
cheap boarding-house food. I wonder what Trigorin will
think of her now?
(*POLINA enters.*)

POLINA: (*Darkly.*) That is the room where your father died,
Nina Mikhailovna. I can always feel it. (*Ominous.*)
When...death has been in a room.

ARKADINA: (*Standing in the bedroom door.*) The mirror is so
dusty, I can hardly see a thing. Why didn't you wipe it?

POLINA: And do you think I'll look in a mirror in a room
where someone's died? Do you want me to see an
apparition?

ARKADINA: You with your silly superstitions! You don't
have to look in the mirror! Just wipe it!

POLINA: And with what must I wipe it, if you please?

ARKADINA: What a moulting old crow! (*Exits to the
bedroom.*)

POLINA: (*Tearful.*) Did you hear what she called me, Nina
Mikhailovna? Did you hear? Do you see how she treats
me? Who does she think she is! Earlier, when I was
helping her up the stairs, she kept saying (*Mimics
ARKADINA.*) 'Don't clutch at me with your claw, don't
poke me with your bony fingers!' Things like that. And
this morning she said I smelled like rancid dripping!
And I can't sleep at night. It's been going on for months.
I'm so tired. As soon as I close my eyes, she calls me.
(*Mimicks ARKADINA.*) 'Polina, Polina!' And never a
please or a thank you! (*Passionate. Talking quietly.*)
Sometimes...Nina Mikhailovna...I want to burn the
house down! Yes! I want to burn it down! I keep seeing

it... Everything going up in flames. And Masha and I sitting in the garden and watching. Just watching. While we eat pineapple preserves!

(*ARKADINA enters with her handbag over her arm and her hat in her hand. Her face is extremely powered and rouged.*)

ARKADINA: (*Putting the hat on the table.*) Well...that feels much better. (*Leans on the table. Gives a little gasp and grimaces.*)

POLINA: What is it?

ARKADINA: Nothing, nothing. Don't stare at me so stupidly! I'm sorry, Polina dear. My nerves...are bad today. It's all the arrangements...and the people.

POLINA: (*Mutters darkly under her breath as ARKADINA continues to speak.*) Arrangements! Ha! She never lifts a finger. I have to do everything as usual. Everything.

ARKADINA: (*To NINA.*) You've heard...haven't you...my darling Kostia's play...is being performed tonight? Isn't that so, Polina dear? (*Walks towards the ottoman.*) Oh, my poor darling , my poor boy. I miss him so. I think about him every day. (*Lies back. Sits and closes here eyes.*) So...many things.

(*The sound of someone whistling tunelessly in the garden.*) That's Trigorin. Just imagine...he's down there...fishing. (*To NINA.*) You must remember... how he loves fishing. He rowed us across, you know. So thoughtful of him. He didn't want me to walk. He said it was too...tiring.

(*The tuneless whistling continues.*) It must be...years since you saw him. (*Little laugh.*) He gets angry with me...when I tease him. I tell him...he never should have become a writer. He should have...dedicated his life to fishing. (*Little laugh.*)

(*The whistling stops. ARKADINA notices that NINA is staring at her.*)

(*To NINA.*) You must find me very changed. No, don't say anything. It's just that...I'm not myself yet. I'm still... convalescing.

(*As ARKADINA continues to speak POLINA leans over and whispers into NINA's ear.*)

POLINA: Convalescing? That's not true. She's dying, Nina Mikhailovna. Dying.

ARKADINA: That's why I've spent months here in the country. Growing...dusty. Losing touch...with everything that's happening...in the world. I've never been able to abide...all this silence...and restfulness. I really don't know what anyone...sees in it. Trigorin...for instance. He...can't get enough of it.

POLINA: (*Sullen.*) I'm sure. With me having to wait on him hand and foot. Ringing for tea any time of the night or day.

ARKADINA: (*Mischievous little smile. To NINA.*) Oh, she's just jealous. She doesn't have an admirer any more, you see. Do you remember Dr Dorn? We all thought he would marry Polina when her husband died. For years and years...as I'm sure you know...they were... What would one call it in polite society? (*Naughty little laugh.*) But then he married a fat widow. And ever since then, Polina has chronic headaches...in fact, she even developed a facial tick. Have you noticed it?

POLINA: (*Jumping up.*) If you weren't so sick I'd go away and never come back! But how can I leave a *dying* woman?

ARKADINA: (*Extremely agitated.*) I'm almost well and you know it! But you can go whenever you like. Go then! Go!!

(*POLINA stomps out.*)

(*Agitated.*) Polina! Polina! (*To NINA.*) Go after her! (*Shrieks.*) Polina! Polina!

(*Pause. POLINA enters and stands silently in the hall entrance.*)

(*Brightly trying to cover.*) I've heard such...nice things about you, Nina. (*Loudly and brightly.*) Haven't we, Polina? About the...splendid work you've been doing in the provinces.

(*As ARKADINA continues to speak, POLINA shakes her head and mutters under her breath. She continues to mutter throughout the following.*)

An acquaintance of mine saw you... Oh, I forget where. She said your performance was extremely...moving.

Of course...all this...naturalism. I always say, if one
wants to be 'natural' one might as well stay at home.
Most disappointing that we haven't seen you in
Petersburg or Moscow. Well...maybe this season or the
next.

NINA: I...don't think so.

ARKADINA: Oh, don't give up so easily, my dear.
These...provincial companies are all very well, but...
they're not what you really want. Am I right? Come and
sit here my dear. Come and sit next to me.
(*She pats the couch. POLINA stops muttering. NINA looks
reluctant, but sits down next to her.*)
You know that tonight when we will be performing my
darling Kostia's play... (*Takes her hand. Urgently.*) You will
be coming won't you? After all...I've come all this way
just to ask you. Kostia...would so have wanted it... It's
such a good sign that you're here. After all...you are the
original cast. Just think...how piquant.
(*POLINA goes to the window and looks out.*)

NINA: I really don't know...

ARKADINA: If it's because you feel a little...awkward...
(*Behind her hand.*) Well...my dear, all that is so far in the
past. I can assure you...Trigorin put it behind him years
ago. He's had so many...affairs of the heart...I don't
even think he can tell them apart. (*Little laugh.*) So you
see...there's no need to think about it. As for me...I
really never took it seriously. (*Little laugh. Suddenly
serious and urgent.*) Come now... I simply won't take no
for an answer. He would have wanted it, you see.
(*The sound of an approaching car.*)

POLINA: (*Darkly.*) Do you hear that? It's Lopakhin's car.

ARKADINA: (*Frightened and tremorous.*) Lopakhin! I
have...a horror of that man! Suddenly appearing out of
nowhere... (Getting *up.*) His father was a serf, you know.
I'm sure he blows his nose on his napkin. Dressed so
dreadfully in black...and always wearing a bowler hat.
(*Becoming more agitated. Moves about restlessly.*) Always...
measuring and pacing in the garden...and around the
house! This morning...I woke up...to find his hideous

face...peering through the window! (*Gives a cry and covers her mouth with her hands.*) I've told him...to go away and stay away! But it's no use. This morning...I found him in the summerhouse...knocking against the walls. (*Very agitated. Almost feverish.*) When I asked...what he was doing...he said the wood was...infested! It couldn't be saved! (*Desperate.*) What... does it have to do with him? Can anyone tell me that? What does it have to do with him?

POLINA: Just stay calm. Trigorin said I must see that you don't get upset. 'We don't want any more hysterics, do we?' That's what he said.

ARKADINA: He would never say anything like that. I don't believe you.

POLINA: I can only tell you what I heard.
(*The car stops.*)

ARKADINA: He's stopped! He's coming here! (*Urgent.*) You mustn't let him in. I really can't bear to see him. (*A loud knock on the front door.*)
(*Whispering. Frightened.*) Tell him to go away...please...please.

LOUD VOICE: (*Calling Off.*) Hullooo! Is anybody here?

ARKADINA: (*Whispering.*) What a voice! Sounds like...the trumpet of doom! (*To POLINA, tugging at her sleeve.*) Go down and tell him Nina Mikhailovna isn't here!

POLINA: She is here. (*Pointing.*) There she is.

VOICE: (*Off.*) Nina Mikhailovna!

ARKADINA: Do what I say! And do it at once! (*Pushing her.*) Go now!

POLINA: I'm going! You don't have to shout! (*Exits. Her footsteps can be heard on the stairs.*)

ARKADINA: (*Sinks down onto the ottoman. Almost cowering.*) I'm sure he wants to buy your estate. He wants to buy up every scrap of land next to the lake. Have you seen (*Gesture.*) the hideous...rash of red-brick villas? And all those vulgar people...
(*The sound of the front door opening slightly and of voices downstairs.*)
(*Whispers.*) Screaming and singing and swimming in our lake! You mustn't sell. Promise me you won't. They'll

overrun us. Overrun us completely. You must have
nothing to do with that man. You have no idea what he is.
(*The sound of the front door closing. POLINA's footsteps can
be heard on the stairs.*)
How can I bear (*Tearful.*) his remorseless...merciless...
persecution?
(*POLINA appears in the door.*)
Is he gone?

POLINA: (*Sullen.*) He'll come back later.

ARKADINA: (*To NINA.*) Then you must send him away.
(*Vague. Distracted.*) I've even had a dream about him. I
dreamt that he drove that...horrid car of his right...
through the house. Smashing...everything in his way.
(*To NINA.*) Ours are the last two estates along the lake,
you know. The very last. (*Short silence.*) I don't hear him
driving away. (*To NINA.*) Did you hear anything?

NINA: No. I don't think so.

ARKADINA: (*Frightened.*) He's here. Lurking. Creeps
about. Measuring! (*To POLINA.*) Look carefully. Can you
see him? (*Almost under her breath.*) What if...he's waiting
for me?

POLINA: (*Looking out of the window.*) There he is. He's
talking to Trigorin.

ARKADINA: (*Sharp intake of breath.*) I've asked him again
and again not to speak to that man!

POLINA: Now they're turning around. They're looking at
the house.

ARKADINA: Step back! Don't let them see you. (*Grimace
of pain. She clutches her side. Almost a wail.*) Why is he
talking to him?

POLINA: Everybody knows. They all...talk about it behind
your back.

ARKADINA: What are you implying?

POLINA: Always making plans for the future. Plotting.
Thick as thieves, they are.

ARKADINA: Are you saying that...Trigorin would betray
me? How dare you? How...dare you?

POLINA: Everyone is talking behind your back! It's time
you opened your eyes!

ARKADINA: Oh... (*Gasps. To NINA.*) What a silly, stupid woman she is. A leech...just like her daughter! Living off me! Sucking me dry! I'm sick and tired of them! They've worn me down. As soon as I'm stronger...I'll leave this place and never come back! The Lopakhin animal can have it all! I don't care! What a relief it will be. Not having...to bury myself in the country. And on top of it all...she treats me abominably! What are you waiting for? Get out of here! Get out!!

POLINA: You call me...stupid! You call me a leech! You chase me out like a dog! But who washes your soiled underwear? Who takes out your slops? At least I've always been good to my Masha! But you treated your son like dirt!!

ARKADINA: Get out!!

POLINA: (*Points upwards.*) There is a higher justice!! A higher justice!! (*Snorts with disgust. Exits.*)

ARKADINA: And close the door behind you!!

(*Sound of POLINA stamping down the stairs and slamming the front door behind her.*)

She's always...at me. Do you see what I mean? Ever since my poor Kostia... (*Gives a small cry and presses her hand in front of her mouth.*) She's been...accusing me. Even if she doesn't say anything. Oh God...the way she looks at me. And that daughter of hers. (*Covers her face with her hands.*) As if I don't know! (*Short silence. Tearful sigh.*) He worshipped me more than any son...ever worshipped his mother. Oh...and I tried to be a good mother to him but after all...I *am* an artist. That is my destiny. He wouldn't understand...that I couldn't be...like other women. He *blamed* me for it. He thought I didn't care about him. Oh, my poor boy. My poor boy. (*Little gasp and then a grimace of pain. Looks around confusedly.*) Where...is my handbag? Where is it? (*Finds the handbag.*) Oh, I thought I'd lost it. (*Opens the handbag with a shaking hand.*) Sometimes...I have a little...twinge. (*Takes out a small bottle of pills.*) ...And then I need...to take this. (*Desperate.*) I can't open it...I can't. (*Opens it.*) There. (*Puts two pills on her tongue. She closes her eyes and*

leans back for the moment. Speaking with her eyes closed.) So
bitter. (*Opens her eyes.*) They always help...quite quickly.
But...when I take them...at night...I can't sleep.
They...make me hear things. It's really...quite peculiar.
Like...voices...whispering. And sometimes...as if
someone is crying and moaning...very close to me.
(*Short silence. Puts the pills back in the handbag.*) I'd...been
away for a whole year. A whole year of playing one
glorious role after another. He'd...written me so many
letters...saying he missed me. And then...at last...when I
arrived...I didn't even greet him. (*Small cry.*) It was the
day after my triumph at Harkov. Never had I had such
an ovation. And that is all I could talk about. Think about
it. If only...if only I'd embraced him. And kissed him.
Said... 'my darling, how I've missed you.' Everything...
would have been...so different. (*Shuddering sigh.*) My
poor...darling boy...thought...I didn't even notice him.
That he was...nothing to me. (*She gives a cry.*) When I saw
him lying there...so pale...and still...I fell down on my
knees beside him and said 'You have taken my life from
me. You have taken my life.' Every day since
then...every day...I have been tortured by regret. But
my public never sees my suffering. Never!
(*NINA sits with her head bowed.*)
(*Tearful.*) I...mustn't get so...emotional. I really...
mustn't. It isn't good for me. I must be well tonight.
It's...Kostia's night. I want everything to be...right for
him. (*She closes the bag with a snap.*) So...you will come
then my dear? Surely you're not going to disappoint me.
I do it for Kostia you see. To give his work...the
recognition it deserves. He would have wanted that.
Surely you must agree? (*Urgently.*) Surely.
(*Short silence.*)

NINA: I will come tonight. Thank you.

ARKADINA: (*Greatly relieved.*) Well...that's settled then.
Kostia was so fond of you. So...fond of you. (*A little gasp
of pain.*)

NINA: What is it?

ARKADINA: Nothing, nothing. (*Short silence. Composes
herself.*) Ever since you were children...you were so

close. Like brother and sister. Oh, I know that...last
summer...he thought he was in love with you. A boy's...
romantic fantasy.

NINA: And I also believed...I loved him. (*Short silence.
Sadly.*) We were...so happy. When he wrote the play...
(*Tuneless whistling from outside.*)
...he said he wrote it for me. He said...if he wrote
it...and I performed it...our spirits would be united.

ARKADINA: For you? Is that so? (*Short silence.*) And here
I was...all these years...thinking he'd written it to please
me. (*Little laugh.*)
(*Tuneless whistling continues.*)
How...deluded can one be? (*Pointedly.*) Isn't that so?
(*Short silence.*)
My dear...won't you just go and see...if that dreadful
Lopakhin is about? I really must go...there's so much to
do. And I don't want to run into him, as you can imagine.
(*NINA goes to the window and looks out.*)

NINA: He's not there.

ARKADINA: (*Pause. Watches NINA.*) Only...Trigorin?

NINA: Yes.

ARKADINA: (*Pause. Watches NINA.*) And what is he doing?

NINA: (*Quietly.*) Fishing.

ARKADINA: Still! (*Little laugh.*)
(*Silence as NINA keeps looking down on TRIGORIN.
ARKADINA watches her intently. The tuneless whistling can
still be heard.*)
(*After a silence.*) Well...then I suppose I can be on my way.

NINA: (*Startled. Turns around quickly. Almost guilty.*) Yes.

ARKADINA: (*Getting up slowly.*) Then...we'll see you about
seven. The play...Or should I say *your* play... (*Little
laugh.*) starts...as I'm sure you know...when the moon
rises. (*Moves rather shakily to the table and puts on her hat.
Stands motionless for a moment then turns suddenly to NINA.*)
Good gracious...I nearly forgot. Trigorin wants to come
up and see you. You won't mind will you? He'd find it so
interesting...to see how changed you are.
(*NINA makes a sound of protest.*)

Oh, come now my dear... (*Moves to the window.*) Surely, you're old friends. No need...to stand on ceremony. (*Leans out and calls down to TRIGORIN.*) My love! (*The whistling stops.*)

Nina so wants to see you! Stop this fishing...and come up at once! Oh look! You've caught an eel. It's still wriggling about! How clever you are, my darling! Now put down that rod...and come up at once! That's a good boy! (*Half turning. Speaking loudly so that TRIGORIN can hear.*) He's coming up, Nina Mikhailovna. He'll be very pleased with himself, I must warn you! He's not caught a fish all summer! (*Leans out.*) In fact...he'll be insufferable! (*Laughs.*)

(*ARKADINA suddenly stops laughing. She turns around slowly. Her face is a mask of pain. She walks slowly and with difficulty to the couch and sits down. She lowers her veil with shaking hands. NINA also seems slightly unsteady on her feet. She leans on the table. Both remain motionless. Sound of the front door being opened. A gust of wind enters the room. it lifts ARKADINA's veil and stirs the feathers on her hat. NINA's hair is blown across her face. They listen to TRIGORIN's footsteps ascending the stairs. The lights fade slowly to black as the footsteps become menacingly louder. The sound of the footsteps can still be heard for a few moments in the black.*)

Pantomime

The sound of the wind intensifies and the pantomime lights fade up. NINA is still standing at the table. Facing front, she is holding a pocket watch by its chain. She is swinging it slowly from side to side, watching it as if mesmerised. She puts it down on the table. She looks sad and forlorn. She glances towards the ottoman and then slowly crosses to it. She stands for a moment, looking lost, then she lies down. As her eyes close, the pantomime lights fade to black. The wind can still be heard in the black.

Scene 4

Lights slowly up. The room is filled with the dark blue shadows of late afternoon. The pocket watch is still on the table. Male voices singing a raucous song accompanied by an accordion can be heard throughout the scene. The singing is heard in the distance and only gets louder when indicated in the text. NINA is lying curled up on the ottoman, sleeping. MASHA is standing near the ottoman, staring at her. She is obviously rather drunk and is swaying slightly. Her hair is extremely dishevelled. She coughs loudly and deliberately. NINA opens her eyes and gives a start.

MASHA: (*Slurring slightly.*) Were you asleep, Nina Mikhailovna?

NINA: (*Sitting up.*) How long have you been standing there?

MASHA I...don't know. Quite long.

(*NINA sighs and drops her head into her hands.*)

NINA: I kept waking up...thinking that I'd had a terrible dream. So terrible...that I'd cried in my sleep. Every time it was about Kostia. That he'd died and that I'd never see him again. And when I realised it was only a dream...I was happy and I'd go back to sleep. (*Cries quietly.*) It kept happening again and again...until I didn't want to sleep anymore. And so...I stayed up all night and only went to sleep when the sun came up. (*Yawns again.*) I can't... seem to wake up. I'm still...half asleep.

MASHA: I also couldn't sleep. I was too excited...about tonight. (*Stumbles and clutches onto the side of the ottoman. Seems about to say something. Opens and shuts her mouth a few times. Seems uncomfortable. Suddenly bursts out.*) I've come to say...something to you, Nina Mikhailovna. I've come...to say something. (*Very distressed.*) I've been practising all day...I've been saying it over and over to myself. (*Sways and steadies herself. Notices NINA looking at her.*) I know what you're thinking. You're thinking: 'Masha, the poor thing... She's drunk again.' But that's not true. I only...had a drop. Just...a drop. Trigorin left some...in his glass...and I thought...if I drink it...then I'll feel...I'll feel...a bit better...

NINA: (*Sadly.*) He...only used to drink French wine and champagne... Now his shoes are stuffed...his cuffs are frayed and he is losing his hair.

MASHA: Because...after...I saw...saw...you...I felt...so bad. I felt...like crying...all the time.

NINA: I'm sorry.

MASHA: So...I only...drank a drop...and now...everything looks...funny. And you (*Points.*) look so faaar away.
(*As they continue to speak, the sound of singing gets slightly louder.*)

NINA: (*Rubbing her forehead.*) My head is so heavy...Feels as if it...can drop off...
(*Far off sound of male voices singing and an accordion being played. The singing is raucous and off-key.*)
(*Lifting her head and listening.*) What's...that?

MASHA: (*Listens.*) People...from the new villas. At night...they sing a lot. When they sing like that...it makes Arkadina cry.

NINA: (*Slight laugh.*) I'm sure.
(*The sound of singing is closer. NINA and MASHA continue to speak over the singing.*)

SONG: There was a young lady from Kharkov
Who liked to take her knickers of
Her knickers off
Her knickers off
Her knickers off
Her knickers off
Who li-ked to take her knickers off!
There was a young lady from Kharkov
Who liked to take her chemise off
Her chemise off
chemise off
chemise off
chemise off
Who li-ked to take her chemise off (*Etc.*)

MASHA: (*Standing perilously on tip-toe and craning her neck to see out.*) Five of them. They have...knotted handkerchiefs on their heads. (*Stumbles.*)

NINA: Masha, why don't you sit down?

MASHA: (*Looks stubborn. Shakes her head. Pause. Suddenly bursts out.*) I have...to say it to you...Nina Mikhailovna ...I have to! You see...you mustn't come tonight! It's not...right Nina Mikhailovna...It's...not right!

NINA: (*Distressed.*) What do you mean?

MASHA: Everything...that happens tonight...is for Kostia. And...for all the people...who want to remember him. The people...who cared about him...and were good to him. So...what would you be doing there? No-one...*hurt* him like...you did! No-one! You don't know...how he... suffered! (*Bows her head. Starts crying almost soundlessly, with an open mouth.*)
(*The singing fades away but continues to be heard in distance.*)
I was glad...when you ran off with that Trigorin. I never thought...you were any good for him. Too full of...fancy ideas. I thought...he'd forget about you. But he didn't. He...thought about you all the time. He only...talked to me...because he wanted to talk about you. Nina this, Nina that, Nina, Nina, Nina! (*Sniffs loudly the takes out her handkerchief and wipes her nose.*)
(*Short silence.*)

NINA: (*Quietly.*) You cared very much for him, didn't you?

MASHA: What if I did? What if I did? I didn't...make a nuisance of myself. I know...I'm plain. I...only wanted to stay close to him... To see...if I could be...of any use. He said...it couldn't be helped. 'That's life,'...he said. But...I hated you...for what you did to him. Thoughts used to...come into my head. I couldn't help it. I couldn't. Terrible...terrible thoughts... (*Speaks in snatches.*) When I heard...Trigorin...left you...I was happy, God forgive me, I was happy! I kept thinking... 'she got what she deserved!' (*Clamps her hand over her mouth and turns away her head.*)
(*Short silence. NINA gets up and goes to the window.*)

NINA: Is that really...what I 'deserved'? Can one 'deserve' anything like that?

MASHA: You didn't see...how he...suffered. Sometimes
I think...God forgive me...that if you...could have loved
him...he might still be alive! He might be out there...
(*Points towards the window.*) opening and closing the
curtains! Seeing that everything is ready... (*Cries.*)

NINA: Don't say that! It's not true! Even if it is...what was
I supposed to do? (*Wipes her palm across her eyes.*) If I only
could have loved Kostia like that. How simple and
happy my life would have been. Do you think I wanted
to fall in love with a man who used to hurt me...and hurt
me? Who didn't care if I lived or died? You don't know
anything! You don't know what I've been through!
(*Tearful laugh.*) That's what everybody says! What a
foolish thing to say! (*Weeps.*)

MASHA: I...don't know what to think Nina Mikhailovna.
I don't know any more. (*Pause. Wipes her nose.*) Every
morning...he'd call me. He'd be...standing at the
window...in his night-shirt...with a letter in his hand.
'Won't you go to town and post this, Masha dear? I've
been writing all night.' And he'd yawn...and rub his
eyes. Always a letter to you. Sometimes...to his mother.
(*Gets up. Seems to be resisting something she needs to say.*)
The day before...he died...he gave me a letter. I
forgot...to post it. It was...the last thing I ever had from
him. I know it wasn't mine...but I kept it. I shouldn't
have...but I kept it. At night...I used to read it...over
and over again. I still...know every word...better than
the Lord's Prayer. But...it wasn't right Nina Mikhailovna.
He wrote it...to you. It doesn't belong to me. I must...
give it back.

NINA: (*Pleading.*) Please Masha...Won't you keep it?

MASHA: (*Getting agitated.*) He wrote it to you! It's for you!

NINA: Of course.

MASHA: (*Moans.*) But I don't have it any more. It became
so thin. It just...blew away. (*Getting excited.*) But...I
can...say it to you! I can do that! I'll do it now.

NINA: But, can't you wait a little? Maybe tomorrow?

MASHA: No. Never put off what you can do now. One never knows what can happen. (*Almost feverish.*) Sit down, Nina Mikhailovna. Sit down.
(*NINA sits reluctantly on the wicker chair near the window.*)
And don't...look at me. (*Closes her eyes and thinks, mutters a few words. Opens her eyes. Slightly slurring her words and swaying a little. Sing-song as if reciting a poem.*) 'Dearest Nina, There is a full moon and it reminds me of you. It is a pale woman looking for (*Falters.*)...a lost country.' (*Pleased.*) You see! I remember it!
(*NINA is deeply moved by the letter.*)
(*As before.*) 'I feel such tenderness for you. I want to kiss your dear eyes and the corners of your mouth. You have lit a flame in my heart that nothing can put out. Not wind or rain or snow. I'm waiting. As always. Your Kostia.
(*NINA looks deeply sad.*)
Are you sad now, Nina Mikhailovna?
(*NINA nods.*)
You mustn't be. Kostia...wouldn't like it. When...he died...I wanted to die too. And I ached all over...as if my bones were broken. But...I never cried. (*Short silence.*) And do you know why, Nina Mikhailovna?
NINA: No.
MASHA: Because...a few weeks before...he came and sat next to me. I was sitting on the bench under the tree and I was crying. He was so gentle. He spoke so softly. He said...and I remember every word... Every word. He said, 'Masha dear, you mustn't drink vodka and be sad all the time. It's not good for you. Won't you try to be just a little happy. Won't you do that for me?' It's the only thing he every asked of me. And I wanted to do it for him. (*Bravely.*) So I've tried never to cry and always to keep my spirits up. But sometimes...I can't help it. I do my best...but I can't help it. The truth is...Nina Mikhailovna... I'm a very...unfortunate person. I have no-one to love me. What can be...more unfortunate than

that? (*Turns her head and looks at NINA. Slightly surprised.*) And so are you, Nina Mikhailovna. Also an unfortunate person.

NINA: (*Quietly.*) Yes. I am.

MASHA: (*Brightening.*) But you...are a more...unfortunate person than I am, Nina Mikhailovna. No-one ever wanted me. But you...threw away your happiness...with your own hands. (*Shakes her head.*) That's very...very unfortunate.

NINA: So...whenever you don't want to be sad...just think of me and count your blessings.

MASHA: (*Contented sigh.*) Yes.

NINA: (*Mock serious.*) And then you can think, 'Nina Mikhailovna, that poor thing. Nowhere...is there another such unfortunate soul.'

MASHA: Not in the whole of Mother Russia.

(*NINA laughs sadly and then stops abruptly. NINA and MASHA stare sadly in front of them. MASHA touches her swollen cheek and groans as the raucous music gets louder and the lights fade slowly to black.*)

Pantomime

As the sound of the wind intensifies, the pantomime lights fade up. NINA is still sitting on the chair near the window. She gets up slowly and stands in front of the window. She looks sad, resigned and completely exhausted. She sinks back onto the chair. Her eyes close, but she starts awake. Very slowly, her eyes close again. Her head slumps onto the arm of the chair as the pantomime lights fade out. The wind can be heard in the black.

Scene 5

The sound of the wind fades out. As the lights fade up on ARKADINA, the room is filled with the soft, uncertain glow of the setting sun. As the lights come up, NINA is asleep on the chair at the window and ARKADINA is standing at the table looking at the pocket watch. She looks extremely dishevelled and is not wearing a hat or carrying a handbag. She is unaware of NINA's presence. She picks up the pocket watch and opens it.

ARKADINA: (*Reading the inscription. Softly and brokenly.*)
'With my eternal love and devotion. Your Arkadina.'
(*A soft cry of distress.*)
(*NINA starts awake. ARKADINA becomes aware of NINA and gasps. Hurriedly she puts the pocket watch back on the table.*)
I didn't hear you. Have you been standing there?
Watching me? And...what did you see, Nina
Mikhailovna? That I'm untidy...and that my hair is
coming down. (*Tries to tidy her hair.*) I've been looking
everywhere for you.

NINA: (*Getting up.*) I've been asleep.

ARKADINA: Don't keep staring at me. You make me
nervous.

NINA: (*Coldly.*) I'm not staring.
(*The stage lights grow dimmer.*)

ARKADINA: It's...suddenly so dark. (*Shivers.*) So cold. It's
clouding over. Just imagine...if it rains tonight. I don't
know what I'll do! It's been...fine every afternoon for a
month...and now this.
(*NINA stands motionless, looking at her.*)
Why must you be so quiet, Nina Mikhailovna? As if...
you're not here at all. (*Short silence.*) I know...I look
frightful. It's because I travelled in that...terrible man's
car. Jolting and bumping...and billowing smoke. And
imagine...my hat was blown right off my head into the
lake. Imported feathers and now it's ruined.
(*Far-off sound of a shutter banging monotonously in the wind.*)
(*Frightened.*) What is that?

NINA: A shutter...banging in the wind.

ARKADINA: Can you imagine, Nina Mikhailovna, can you
imagine...that I had to ask that oafish Lopakhin to bring
me here. That I had to...beg him for a favour. I actually
called him *Mister* Lopakhin. I said...I had to see you
urgently...urgently. He'll be coming back for me soon.
(*Lights grow brighter again.*)

Well…maybe it's clearing. I can…only hope for the best. Some guests…have arrived much too early. I find it…so ill-mannered. Quite unexcusable. (*Awkward silence.*) Well…as I said…I wanted to ask you something. I want to know…if you've decided to come tonight. You…seemed a little uncertain.

NINA: I said I was coming, Madame.

ARKADINA: I'm afraid…and I must apologise…I feel I was rather insistent. I don't want to place you under any obligation. I want you to feel…quite free to do as you please.

NINA: Thank you.

(*Short silence. The shutter can be heard banging in the wind.*)

ARKADINA: (*Emphatic.*) So…if you'd rather not come…I'll understand completely!

NINA: Have you changed your mind Madame? Is that what you're trying to say? Would you prefer if I stayed away?

ARKADINA: Of course not. You misunderstood me completely. It's just that I felt I'd been insensitive and I wanted to apologise. Of course, you're more than welcome. That goes without saying. (*Little laugh.*) You silly girl.

NINA: Thank you.

ARKADINA: Oh well…that's settled then.

(*The lights dim. The shutter can no longer be heard.*)

How gloomy it's becoming. So gloomy and cold. I can hardly bear the thought of getting into that car again. I can hardly bear it. Of course he drives like a demon. You can't imagine. And all the way he broke wind. Really disgusting. And he did it quite openly. Oh I feel so light-headed. I think I'm going to have to sit down. (*Gropes her way to the chair near the window. while NINA watches her impassively. She sits down. Short silence.*) It's…so difficult for me…I do hope you won't be angry…but the truth is…Nina Mikhailovna…The truth is…that you were quite right about me…changing my mind. I hope you'll forgive me…but the fact is…that I've decided…it won't be quite…appropriate for you to come tonight. (*Short silence.*) I'm terribly sorry. (*Gets up unsteadily.*) But...I think it will be for the best.

NINA: I'll only see the play. Naturally...I won't stay afterwards. I don't expect you to entertain me.

ARKADINA: (*Gives a little gasp and sits down again. Presses her palms to her temples.*) You are forcing me...to explain myself...Nina Mikhailovna. I am Arkadina! You must know...how difficult it is for me! You stand there... looking at me. With those...eyes of yours. (*Distressed.*) What...do you expect me to say? (*Angry sarcasm.*) Stay away tonight! I beg you! I'll go down on my knees if you want me to! Is that what you want?

NINA: No. Of course not. If you'll only tell me why?

ARKADINA: (*Slight cry.*) I'm not very well! (*Fragile and tremulous.*) If only you knew...what I've been through these last months. So helpless...so weak...so frightened! Then...maybe...you'll have mercy on me! (*Little cry.*) After all...I'm not asking for very much!

NINA: I'm sorry, but I want to know why? Surely you can understand that?

ARKADINA: What more do you want me to say? I couldn't rest this afternoon...I have to rest in the afternoons...I'm still not very strong...I...kept remembering...I kept seeing everything over and over again... (*Passes her hand over her eyes.*) The last time... when the play was performed... The same time of the year... Everything...just the same. When you came on the stage...in your white dress...your long hair...and so... young! Trigorin's eyes never left your face... And from that moment...that very moment...he started drawing away from me... (*Gasps.*) And of course later... when he left me... Well, my dear...I must confess that I was... very...distressed. There had been others, of course ...but with you... Well...he seemed to be rather...more serious. Naturally...I did think it would pass...but how can one ever be sure? (*Strange little laugh.*) You see... The first time we met I knew...he was the only man for me. I'd never really cared about a man before. I mean

Kostia's father was just a Vaudeville artiste. A
ventriloquist! With a dummy! What would I do without
Trigorin? What would I do?

NINA: I'm so sorry if I caused you distress in the past. I
didn't mean to.

ARKADINA: (*Getting up. Disdainful.*) You hardly need to
feel sorry my dear. Hardly. After all he came back to me,
didn't he? It was you who couldn't keep him. You lost
him because you didn't understand him. You could
hardly appreciate a man like that. You thought he wanted
love and fidelity. But you see, my dear... (*Little laugh.*)
he's an artist. He can't bear too much reality. (*Grimace of
pain. Closes her eyes.*)

NINA: (*Distressed.*) But why are you telling me this?

ARKADINA: I never showed Trigorin how he hurt me.
Feelings are not what he wants from me. What he wants
...is the actress... Admired...vain...glorious! It is my
best part. (*Grand gesture.*) And I play it...consummately!
(*Turns her face away. A grimace of pain.*)

NINA: (*Getting up, very agitated.*) It doesn't matter anymore!
I don't care! I only want to get some rest! (*Moves towards
the bedroom.*) I travelled all night. So far. And I never got
any sleep on the train.

ARKADINA: You've always been a little hypocrite! Earlier
the two of you were so...polite...talking about...this...
and that. Do you think I'm blind? Do you think I didn't
see the looks that he was giving you? And you...all
modesty and lowered eyes! (*Imitating TRIGORIN.*) 'Nina
Mikhailovna has become so fragile. Did you notice her
delicate wrists? What a sweet spirit she has.' (*Gasps.
Presses her hand to her mouth.*) Because I'm not strong...
because I've been ill...because I'm...older now, a little
older, you think it will be...so easy. (*Gasps for breath.*)
This time...if he leaves...it would kill me, Nina
Mikhailovna...It... (*Faltering.*) would...

NINA: Please don't distress yourself. If you don't want me
to come tonight, I won't.

ARKADINA: You...won't?
(*The shutter can be heard banging in the wind.*)

NINA: No.

ARKADINA: Are you sure?

NINA: I promise.

ARKADINA: (*Leading NINA to the window.*) You could watch from here. You can see the stage quite clearly.

NINA: Yes. I'll do that.

(*Short silence.*)

ARKADINA: Well...Nina Mikhailovna...You've been most understanding...most gracious...I'm sorry I've not been myself...I've got this terrible ringing in my ears.

(*Sound of car approaching.*)

There he is. I mustn't keep him waiting. I hope...I've not been gone too long...I...don't want anyone to notice. (*Rises unsteadily.*) Did I bring anything with me? No...it was only my hat.

NINA: And I also want to tell you that...I'll be leaving very soon.

ARKADINA: Will you? (*Short silence.*) Oh well...I suppose there isn't anything here for you.

NINA: (*Quietly.*) No.

(*Loud sound of honking.*)

ARKADINA: (*Fearful. Closing both her ears with her hands.*) What a terrible sound! What a terrible sound! (*Drops her hands. Tearful. Seems unsteady on her feet.*) He can't even...call for me at the door. How dreadfully... ill-mannered. And now I suppose I will have to...be grateful. (*Sees TRIGORIN's pocket-watch on the chair. With extreme sarcasm.*) I saw that...he left his...pocket watch behind... One of his old tricks! (*Crosses to the chair.*) And later he'll...come back to fetch it! (*Grabs the pocket-watch.*) I'm so sick...and tired...of his vile lies and deceit! I could smash it to pieces! Stamp on it!

(*Sound of honking. ARKADINA sways. NINA puts a hand under her elbow to steady her.*)

Thank you. (*Takes a few steps towards the door with NINA still holding her arm. Frees her arm with dignity.*) I can manage from here. Well...my dear...please let me know if I can do anything for you. And when you're in Moscow...you must come back-stage...and praise me.

(*Little laugh.*)

NINA: Thank you.

ARKADINA: (*In the door.*) Until then...*Au revoir.* (*Exits unsteadily.*)

(*NINA stands sadly looking after her with a look of profound sadness. Loud sound of honking.*)

(*Off. Almost a bird-like screech.*) I'm coming! I'm coming! (*NINA sinks down onto the ottoman. She starts sobbing heartbrokenly and covers her face with her hands. The lights fade to black as the shutter can still be heard banging in the wind. In the black the sound of the wind fades up.*)

Pantomime

As the sound of the wind intensifies, the pantomime lights fade up. NINA is still sitting on the ottoman. She blinks and opens her eyes as if she's just woken up. She looks about her and gets up slowly. Her expression and her movements suggest a poignant and gentle sadness. She looks at the room as if seeing it for the last time. She moves to the bedroom entrance and stands there for a moment, looking in. She turns and moves to the table. Almost tenderly, she closes the story book. She carries it to the ottoman, lifts the seat and puts it inside. She closes the ottoman slowly, stands motionless for a moment and then moves to the window where she stands looking out as the lights fade out. The wind can be heard in the black.

Scene 6

Early evening. The lights as in Scene 1. The wind can be heard throughout the scene. Lights slowly up. NINA is standing in front of the window looking out. Nina's MOTHER is standing in the corner, back left, watching her. At first there is silence and a fragile tension in the air.

NINA: (*Haltingly.*) Since I've come back...everything... seems so forlorn...and forgotten. Strange how changed they all are. Strange. Nothing...as I remember it. I don't even know if I'm awake. (*Passes her palm over her eyes.*)

(*MOTHER gives a long drawn-out, slightly vocalised, sigh.*)

There is Arkadina...and Masha...and Polina...and
Trigorin, with a red handkerchief in his breast-pocket.
(*Short silence.*) When Trigorin came to see me today,
Mother, I was so afraid. I was afraid that it would give
me pain. That I might...start loving him again...as
desperately as I used to. But when he came in...all
I thought was 'Where is Trigorin? This can't be him.' All
I could see was a man with dirty cuffs who kept fidgeting
with his necktie...trying not to meet my eyes...and
talking...about trivial things. (*Short silence.*) He seemed
...like a stranger. And I couldn't imagine...that I ever
had any feelings for him.

MOTHER: (*Sighs.*) Everyone changes. Everyone changes...
Except me.

NINA: (*Short silence.*) And there is the young actress...
waiting in the wings. They can't see her, but I can.
I wonder if her heart is racing? If she's...trembling as I
was? Waiting for the play to begin. Waiting...to be seen
by such...important people. By...Trigorin. (*Short silence.*)
Now...only the moon has to rise and then...her
dress...her hair... Like watching myself all those years
ago. (*Short silence.*) After it was over...I ran home
through the trees. I knew that something had...happened
to me. That my life would never be the same. 'Trigorin,
Trigorin, Trigorin.' I kept repeating over and over again.
I looked up and saw that the stars had become...almost
unbearably bright. The lake was shining. It was lighter
than the sky. (*Short silence.*) Now everything seems so
dim...and gloomy. Even...the air is heavy...and difficult
to breathe. (*Forlorn.*) And the water looks black...and
cold...and deep. Where...is the beautiful place...where I
was young and happy?

MOTHER: Don't tell me... Don't tell me any more! I don't
want to hear about the water. And come away from the
window! (*Moans.*) Oh...oh...oh. All day...this terrible
wind. I can't bear it. And this draughty house. Can you
feel it? The cold air? Where is it coming from? It must
be blowing through the cracks. (*Shivers.*) They seem to be
getting wider and wider.

NINA: (*Half-turns to her MOTHER.*) A little earlier...I had a strange dream.

MOTHER: I wish I could have a dream. Wish I could. I would be so happy. Sometimes I close my eyes (*Closes her eyes.*) and try to remember your father's face when he used to call me his 'sweet girl' and feed me glazed fruit from Germany. But when I open my eyes...I'm back here. And I'm alone. Oh...oh...and I'm cold. Always cold... And about...to have a headache.
(*The sound of the wind becomes slightly louder.*)
Oh, the wind is getting stronger. I'm afraid it's going to blow the house into the lake.

NINA: (*Soothingly, still looking out.*) It won't, Mother. It won't. (*Pause.*) I dreamt about Kostia. I woke up... Then I saw him standing next to me. He looked at me...so tenderly. I knew he didn't want me to be sad anymore. He leaned forward and spoke to me. He spoke...very slowly and seriously. He said, '*You* are the dreamer of the dream. And you can dream *anything.*' And since then my heart has felt so light. So...light.
(*The loud sound of wind.*)

MOTHER: (*A little cry.*) Oh... Oh...I'm so frightened...

NINA: (*Still looking out.*) Don't be frightened, Mother. You don't have to be frightened.

MOTHER: I'm frightened... Frightened... Oh...oh...
(*She exits back left, unseen by NINA.*)

NINA: (*Still looking out.*) Arkadina is fanning herself with a feather fan... Polina is holding the ear-trumpet up to her ear...and there is Masha...sitting on a kitchen chair. (*Pause.*) All the people seem to be talking. Trigorin is throwing his head back...his mouth is wide open...and he is laughing. (*Short silence. Strains to hear.*) But why...can't I hear anything? (*Moves slightly forward and listens intensely, but continues to seem confused.*) I...can't hear anything. Not a sound. (*Little gasp.*) Only...my own breath. And my heart...beating. Everything...seems so silent...so sad. So...far away. (*Short silence. Gentle intake of breath.*) The moon is rising. A huge...red moon.

(The breeze is still ruffling NINA's hair. As NINA continues to speak, the sound of the wind grows louder and louder.)
Suddenly a strong breeze is rippling the water. It's growing stronger and stronger! There were waves on the lake! Madame Arkadina's fan is blown out of her hand! Polina clutches her shawl! Trigorin tries to catch his cravat! Masha is blown right off her chair! The actress is swept off her feet!
(The wings start flapping and billowing. The sound of the wind is very loud now. NINA has to shout to make herself heard.)
And now...look!! Look!! The little stage is rising into the air!! It's hovering there over the water!! Now...it's spreading its wings...and flying away!!
(Wide-eyed, NINA watches the stage as it flies higher and higher into the air. She continues to watch as the sound of the wind becomes extremely loud. Quite softly, underneath the wind, music can now be heard. Cross fade as the rest of the stage becomes dark and a single beam of light illuminates NINA's face. The music becomes louder and louder until it drowns out the sound of the wind. The music, played on cello, accordion and flute, is enchanting and joyous.
Although the wind can no longer be heard, NINA's hair is still being moved and lifted by the wind. Her expression has changed to one of wonderment and, as the light fade very slowly to black, to ecstatic surrender.
The music can still be heard for some moments in the black.)

The End.

www.ingramcontent.com/pod-product-compliance
Ingram Content Group UK Ltd.
Pitfield, Milton Keynes, MK11 3LW, UK
UKHW020721280225
455688UK00012B/454